To: Marlene

From: Roy + Jea

Alice Hoffman

Alice Hoffman

Queen of Bogue Banks

Kathleen McMillan Guthrie

Heritage Dance Foundation®
Director of Education
Melissa Grimes Zwerling
107 South Center Street
Goldsboro, NC 27534
www.ballroom.org

ISBN: 978-0-9961954-0-9
Library of Congress Control Number: 2015949622

10 9 8 7 6 5 4 3 2 1 2 1 1 1 5

Drawings by Kathleen McMillan Guthrie
Cover Design by Heather Gugliotta

Printed in the United States of America

∞This paper meets the requirements of ANSI/NISO Z39.48-1992 (Permanence of Paper)

For Douglas, who fishes in the sea

Our deference, humility, and respect toward Mother Nature have been lost in the dense fog of our self-perceived invincibility.

Is there hope, or are we to remain blind and deaf to the signs and calls of nature?

As we stand on the beach looking at the present of our feet and gazing at the horizon of our future, we must wonder: Is this to be the last beach?

From *The Last Beach*

My home is a paradise lost.

D.G.

ACKNOWLEDGMENTS

I thank Dr. Charles Zwerling; without his interest, enthusiasm, and support, this work would have remained on a shelf in my bookcase.

I thank my husband, Douglas, who has been with me all these years. I thank my children, Chad and Heather, who helped me take notes, listened to me, and gave me helpful criticism. My love to you.

I thank "Cap't" Jim Willis for his much needed information. He knows more about Bogue Banks than anyone.

I thank Max Gugliotta for two excellent ideas that I used with his approval.

I thank Mr. David Parker for his professional advice, patience, and perseverance.

I thank my sister, Jill, for reading this work and giving valuable advice.

I thank Mr. John Matthias for permission to use his poem.

I thank BookLogix for the professionalism and response to questions and problems.

I thank people who remembered things about Alice Hoffman and Salter Path and willingly told me whatever they could think of and often supplied pictures.

I remember with fondness Col. Charles O. Pitts, my first college history professor who became my good friend. I hope we meet again.

Here's to you, Larry.

TABLE OF CONTENTS

Preface to 2015 Edition

I was in the manuscript room at East Carolina University, searching through the card catalog (like *Star Wars*, this was "a long time ago in a galaxy far, far away"), looking for certain material for some paper I had to write for some class, and I kept coming across Alice Hoffman and Bogue Banks in the files. Alice Hoffman. Alice Hoffman. Wait a minute. The Alice Hoffman who had owned half of Bogue Banks, including my village, Salter Path? I had heard stories about her from my husband (who as a four-year-old feared her), and other people in Salter Path who had dealt with her in various capacities. What were these opinions? She was mean; no, she was good. She was afraid of thunderstorms. She loved to sue people. She was uppity. She loved Bogue Banks; no, she didn't. She was a rich Yankee. She was a German spy in World War II. She was a Roosevelt; no, she wasn't. Why was she in the card catalog?

Well, she was dead and had left her correspondence to the library at ECU. Forty-four big boxes filled with letters, bills, legal documents, pictures, a partial autobiography, and on and on. I asked for box number one, folder A, signed for it, sat down at a table, and began to read. I was hooked. I couldn't let one piece of paper go by without reading it. I began to make notes (notes on index cards with a pencil!) I returned again and again, reading, note-taking, copying (many, many dimes fed into the copier). My children helped me at times (I still have notes in their handwritings). What to do with all this information?

As an undergrad in history, I wrote a short paper about Hoffman for a class on the New South. I kept reading in the manuscript room, and in the midst of this, Frank Wooten Jr., an attorney from Greenville, North Carolina, died and left *his* papers to ECU. Four of his boxes had to do with Alice Hoffman, as he had been her (last in a long line) attorney. More reading and note-taking about this New York City woman.

I continued school and received a master's degree in history. My thesis was on, you'll never guess, Alice Hoffman. For some strange reason, I knew more about her than anyone else. Why? To what end? I spoke to a few groups here in Carteret County about her, but that was all. I put all the notes and copies, all the research in a large box and hauled it up to my attic. Mostly I taught history part time, and then English and Literature for different universities. My parents died, my sister-in-law, Violet Ann, too. Children moved away, moved home. I took care of my family, had three delightful grandchildren, gardened, cleaned house, fished, went out in the boat, learned some art, lived life, got older. You know, good and bad, hot days and cold days, rain and shine.

But then a friend, Chip Zwerling, said to me one day a while ago, "What's this I hear about you having a thesis?" I said, "Yes, I wrote one about a woman, Alice Hoffman. I've got a copy at home." He said he would like to see it, so I lent it to him. The next thing I knew he had mailed it off to Georgia, and here we are. It's been most surprising to me, as that was a different time, a different Salter Path, a different world, a different me.

Now, the reason for this preface is twofold. More needs to be said about the original work, and I want to name two main themes that manifest in Alice Hoffman's story.

First, Hoffman attempted to live "in a man's world." Much of feminism does not attract me, but fair is fair no matter the time and place, and Alice Hoffman conducted her life unlike many women did then. She married, because to be divorced was more socially acceptable than to have never married. She schooled herself as best she could in law, business, property management, and farming, although she should have taken more advice from authorities and experts. She often flouted convention. She pleased herself. Did the way she was raised, the manner in which she fashioned her life, lead her to pursue the eviction of an entire village in 1923?

Second, the old, old American story of North versus South is obvious. Before its foundation in 1776, the United States moved toward the Civil War of 1861–65, as the two regions developed differently; one forging ahead in industry and mercantilism, the other remaining by and large agricultural. The Civil War did not mend the relationship between North and South nor bring them closer together, and well into the twentieth century, they continued to be unfriendly, even hostile.

Reflecting this larger regional hostility was a smaller struggle between New Yorker Alice Hoffman and the people of Carteret County, North Carolina. They hindered this Northern woman from controlling a large chunk of land any way she saw fit. Stop hunting on her property? No. Share fishing from her beaches? No. Evict families from their ancestral home that she had acquired? No. Not then, not there. Did the many years of freedom and isolation lead the men of Salter Path, a small fishing village, to resist Hoffman?

Just as the years 1861–65 were the culmination of national strife, so the year of 1923 was the crux of the conflict between Alice Hoffman and Salter Path. Here is the story of a New York City socialite and a community of Banks fishermen. Think on it.

Kathleen Guthrie

Salter Path, NC

April 2015

Preface

Alice Hoffman, born in 1862 in New York City, lived on Bogue Banks in Carteret County, North Carolina, for many years and became a part of its local legend. This work describes Hoffman's entire life, but centers on events in Carteret County.

Hoffman's complete correspondence–financial papers, legal documents, farm records, and partial autobiography, located in Joyner Library at East Carolina University in Greenville, North Carolina–is the primary source for this study. Hoffman wrote the autobiography in the latter part of her life, and although it provides a background for her younger years, it also reflects an ostentatious personality. The correspondence and documents in the collection reveal a more candid picture.

The first chapter, however, is drawn largely from Hoffman's autobiography. In it, she reminisces about events, people, and difficulties that were important to her. The fourth chapter was pieced together with great difficulty. Court records of the many lawsuits that make up that chapter's story were kept in a haphazard and careless manner. If not for the additional support of the Frank M. Wooten Jr. Papers, donated to the Manuscript Collection in the summer of 1993, the task may have been impossible. Wooten, a deceased attorney from Greenville, North Carolina, represented Hoffman for many years. The papers of Carteret County lawyers, Julius F. Duncan, E.H. Gorham, and Claude Wheatly, which could have supplied additional sources for this thesis, had been destroyed.

Because I have arranged this thesis topically and geographically, some overlapping of time periods occurs. The chronology in Appendix B clarifies certain important events in Hoffman's life.

The many troubles between Hoffman and the villagers of Salter Path, North Carolina, have become the subject of poetry, which is included in Appendix E.

Photo Gallery

Alice Hoffman, age eighteen.
Courtesy of Connie Willis.

Hoffman circa 1890.

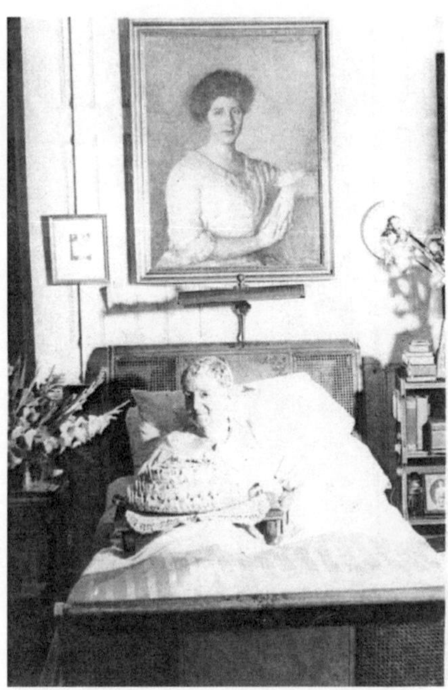

Hoffman on her ninetieth birthday.
Courtesy of Connie Willis.

No. 1006 FIFTH AVENUE

One of Hoffman's Manhattan buildings.
Courtesy of Connie Willis.

Shore House, Hoffman's Bogue Banks home.
Courtesy of Connie Willis.

The living room at Shore House.
Courtesy of Connie Willis.

Hoffman's Tea House on Bogue Banks where she entertained guests.
Courtesy of Connie Willis.

One of Hoffman's china services brought to Shore House from New York City.
Courtesy of Connie Willis.

Gabrielle Brard, Hoffman's French companion.
Courtesy of Connie Willis.

Brard at Shore House. Note the sign above her.
Courtesy of Connie Willis.

Sign Hoffman erected on the road to her North Carolina home.
Salter Path men shot out the "No."

Salter Path Fishing Crew, 1926.
The News & Observer, Volume CXXIII. No. 123, May 2, 1926.

Red Bird Crew circa 1950.

Salter Path Fishing Crew circa 1955.

Frost Fishing Crew, 1994.

David John Willis mending net.
The News & Observer, Volume CXXIII. No. 123, May 2, 1926.

Kenneth Moore with mullet catch circa 1940s.

Tea House Fish Camp circa 1940s.

Flora Bell Pittman and Rita Guthrie hanging laundry at McClamrock Fish Camp circa 1940s.

"Piggy" George Lewis and Sam Salter bringing fish ashore circa 1940s.

Alex Guthrie and Stacy Willis loading fish on truck circa 1940s.

Launching the dory through the surf, 1994. Courtesy of Diane Hardy.

Pulling in the net, 1994. Courtesy of Diane Hardy.

Waiting to tie on the net, 1994. Courtesy of Diane Hardy.

A good haul of mullet, 1994. Courtesy of Diane Hardy.

Fishing on into the night circa 1990s.

Another good haul of mullet, 2014. Courtesy of Heather Gugliotta.

The News & Observer, Volume CXXIII.
No. 123, May 2, 1926.

A view of Salter Path from the ocean side circa 1940s.

Salter Path school children in front of church circa 1927.

Road along shore in Salter Path circa 1920s.

First Methodist Church in Salter Path that burned down in the early 1940s.

First Methodist Church, Salter Path.

The mail boat delivered mail to Salter Path for many years.

Salter Path circa 1930s.

Jimmy and Flora Bell Pittman's house circa 1940s.

Charlie and Sarah Salter.
Salter argued over a cow with John Glover of Atlantic Beach.
They apparently shot and killed one another
and were found dead the next day on Hog Hill, 1917.

Flora Bell Smith and Minnie Willis circa 1930s.

Harvey Willis and Alexander (Uncle Crick) Willis circa 1930s.

Salter Path School circa 1940s.

Dick Willis's store circa 1930s.

Albert and Addie Guthrie.
Courtesy of Ronald Smith.

People on porch circa 1940s.
Courtesy of Ronald Smith.

Salter Path Post Office.
Jean Smith was Postmistress and ran the office from her home.
Courtesy of Ronald Smith.

Thomas Guthrie and Velna Grey Willis circa 1950s.

Adrienne Moore of Salter Path worked for Hoffman at Shore House, 1950.
Courtesy of Connie Willis.

Homer's Point circa 1950s.

David John and Em Willis.
Courtesy of Ronald Smith.

Salter Path children, 1952.

Salter Path circa 1950s.

Henry Frost fishing on the beach, 2014.
Courtesy of Heather Gugliotta.

Douglas Guthrie throwing stingray back into the water
that had been caught in the net, 2014.
Courtesy of Heather Gugliotta.

Chapter One

New York, Paris, China, and Canada

n the extreme southern end of the chain of barrier islands known as the Outer Banks of North Carolina lies Bogue Banks, tucked behind Cape Lookout. The island, now commercially developed and completely populated, remained remote and isolated until the mid-twentieth century. Two large tracts of land escaped development: Fort Macon State Park on the island's eastern end and the North Carolina Aquarium, two hundred ninety-eight acres of wooded property located in the center of the island. Although many inhabitants of Carteret County, which includes Bogue Banks, might recognize her name, few know much about Alice Hoffman. Recalled as a benefactor, conservationist, and lover of the island, this eccentric New Yorker, "Queen of Bogue Banks," manifested a different woman.

Hoffman, born during the Civil War years and shaped by a changing America, developed into an unusual woman. On the fringe of the powerful Northeastern elite, wealthy, but not of the "old" money, she followed the customs of that class, which included education, travel, and the trappings of the "good life." Hoffman, however, rejected the accepted and approved role of woman as wife and mother. She spent a fair amount of her energies in the male-dominated world of business. Hoffman, also involved in numerous legal contests, spent enormous amounts of time and money in various courts of law. Rumor said that "she would rather go to court than to the theatre."[1]

Perhaps influenced by components of the Progressive Movement, Hoffman supported women's suffrage and donated money for urban improvement, but molded by upper class behavior during the earlier Gilded Age, Hoffman rejected any type of progressive social gospel that caused concern for the underprivileged. Unlike fellow New Yorker Theodore Roosevelt, a leader of national progressivism, born four years before Hoffman into a well-to-do mercantile and banking family, Hoffman never "acquired a compulsion to do good for people less fortunate."[2] Hoffman, rather, desired to increase her own wealth and wanted to leave something tangible to those who would follow. To that end, Hoffman bought properties, including her estate on Bogue Banks, hoping that land, unlike ephemeral investments, would last. In that, she was wrong. Hoffman's North Carolina acres, as well as her other properties, caused her no end of troubles.

Born on June 8, 1862 in her grandfather's house on the south side of 34th Street in New York City, New York, Hoffman considered the address to be "one of the places to be born, socially speaking."[3] Some years later, E. Idell Zeisloft, editor of *The New Metropolis*, categorized the people of Manhattan Island into seven classes: "The very rich, the rich, the prosperous, the well-to-do comfortable, the well-to-do uncomfortable, the comfortable or contented poor, and the submerged or uncomfortable poor."[4] Hoffman, apparently, belonged to Zeisloft's rich or prosperous class. Granddaughter of Theron R. Butler, a wealthy New York City merchant, and daughter of Albert W. Green, owner of a furniture and department store, the Green-Joyce Company, Hoffman would later be the aunt of Eleanor Butler Roosevelt, wife of Theodore Roosevelt Jr.,[5] as well as a cousin of Ohio Supreme Court Justices Edward G. Matthias, and his son, John Marshall Matthias. John Matthias would play a prominent role in Hoffman's later years.

At an early age, Hoffman displayed a strong streak of independence. Hoffman's mother, writing to her sister, assessed the new daughter in 1864:

> I determined to write a good long letter with ink but unfortunately Alice has been having a stubborn streak this evening and I had to whip her hard . . . so that my hand trembles so with the excitement, that I concluded to dispense with ink and use pencil. Poor little thing she had a hard time and so did I but I finally conquered her.[6]

Despite such expressions of parental authority, Hoffman's parents ignored her demonstrations of temper, because they thought she had a weak heart. At eight years of age, thin and pale, Hoffman traveled with her father to his parents' home in Ohio. Left there for an extended visit, Hoffman often went without shoes and stockings on her grandparents' farm. When her parents returned for her, she looked so healthy and robust that her mother exclaimed: "Take all your clothes off, if you want to . . . if taking off your shoes and stockings has made you look like this!"[7]

Hoffman's aunt, Helena Butler, undertook Hoffman's education until the age of eight. Butler had decided many years before that American women needed political education. She successfully persuaded a Harvard professor to teach six members of her growing organization, The League for the Political Education of Women. These classes quickly expanded until three thousand women were taught at various locations. At an early age, Hoffman encountered her aunt's reforming feminist interests which undoubtedly influenced the young girl.

At this time, Hoffman's mother died after the birth of a third daughter, and Hoffman moved with her two sisters into her grandfather's house at 433 Fifth Avenue, New York City, New York. She had to part with her beloved childhood nurse, Nathalie, the only link to her mother. Her maternal grandparents and her mother's only sister raised her, as her father was frequently away on business. Through childhood memories, Hoffman later remembered that, whenever in New York City, her father spent every Sunday at his wife's grave on a beautiful knoll in Greenwood Cemetery.

After the move to her grandfather's house, Hoffman attended the Williams's school next door. Her willful disposition continued to develop and she recalled:

> I must have been a funny child, for I removed [anyone] from my heart without the least compunction, no matter what the previous degree of intimacy had been if I thought that they deliberately tried to hurt me. Once playing with a group of children in West 38-th Street, my most intimate friend said: 'You ought to hear what your grandmother told my mother about you.'
>
> I walked right up to the sitting-room where my grandmother was looking out of the window, and demanded an explanation. She, taken unawares, was at a loss to understand, 'If I did not know that Mrs. R. was a lady, I would ask her for an explanation,' and there it remained. But from that moment, my friend no longer counted with me. Her mother brought her to see me, and my grandmother took me downstairs where we sat in silence and looked at one another, while our elders made conversation, for we had nothing further in common. She had wished to wound me and had succeeded. There was no more to be said about it.[8]

Hoffman's wealthy family, part of the New York elite, taught her the etiquette of polite society. Their social conversation focused on the superficial. In this age of American Victorianism, "money and sex were never discussed, and ladies were not supposed even to think about them. . . . Not only did one not express feeling, one did not even discuss it.[9]

Owing perhaps to her mother's early death, Hoffman continued to develop into a headstrong young woman. Tall and strong, with a creamy complexion and thick, unruly dark hair, Hoffman enjoyed both intellectual and physical exercise. A friend wrote a poem to her:

A queenly air,
A stately grace.
Diana's form,
And Juno's face,
A heart that's true,
And has no malice,
The whole divine,
And your hair, Alice.[10]

Privileged to receive an education owing to her societal class and money, Hoffman attended Mrs. Porter's School for Girls in Farmington, Connecticut, administered by a sister of the president of Yale College. There, she became an accomplished pianist and perfected her singing voice. She mastered French, German, and Swedish, understood both Spanish and Italian, studied political economy and the history of art, and read Noah Porter's book *The History of Philosophy*, on the science of the human intellect and moral philosophy. She did not receive business or legal training, reserved only for men.

Hoffman spent summers with sisters, grandparents, and an aunt at Profile House, a luxurious hotel in the White Mountains of Maine. She took frequent trips to Bar Harbor on the Atlantic coast, but she hated these vacations, as she was expected to mix with company, walk, play tennis, and dance. In the evenings, amidst tables filled by groups of fashionably dressed, respectable people, Hoffman played whist and bridge. Hoffman loved the out-of-doors, preferring horseback riding and sailing to physical exercise. One summer at Bar Harbor, a handsome man proposed marriage to Hoffman. She rejected his proposal, explaining that she wanted to travel, study, and "be something" other than a housewife and mother.[11]

Before her twenty-first birthday, Hoffman's father, then in Columbus, Ohio, decided to return to the New York City area. Albert Green had established a successful department store in Columbus, the Green-Joyce Company. He planned to build another store in New York. Hoffman and her sisters moved with him into a home of their own at 114 Harrison Street in East Orange, New Jersey. Green had an atypical view concerning the rights and duties of women. Despite discouraging his daughters from marrying, Alice had a brief marriage to musician John Ellis Hoffman, a Bostonian, which ended in divorce in 1911. Later, she agreed with her father: "Next to the inestimable treasure of the real love which exists, though so difficult to achieve, I have always considered my personal liberty as my most precious possession."[12] Hoffman only mentioned her husband in her autobiography once, and as none of their letters are included in her papers, she very well may have destroyed any correspondence between them.[13]

Albert Green's attitude toward women exerted a strong influence on his other two daughters as well. Alexandra, Hoffman's older sister, married but remained childless. Grace, her younger sister, married Henry Alexander, divorced him, remarried him, and permanently divorced him again. Grace was the only one of the three sisters to bear a child. Her daughter, Eleanor Butler Alexander, married Theodore Roosevelt, Jr., eldest son of President Theodore Roosevelt. They had four children.

Shortly after Hoffman moved to New Jersey with her father and sisters, her grandfather died, leaving her mother's share of his estate to her. She thus became independently wealthy before the age of twenty-one. Soon after, upon the death of her father, she received a third of his estate as well. Through her inheritances, she became a partner in the United States Trust Company of New York and the Saving Investment and Trust Company of New Jersey. Hoffman held stock in the New York Railways and the Lake Shore Railway Company, received dividends from surface roads, and collected rent from buildings in New York City. She benefited from her late grandfather's investments in the industrialization of the South, owning shares in several Southern cotton mills.[14]

Hoffman made several trips to Europe in the latter half of the 1800s, accompanied by family and friends. On her first European excursion, she traveled with a friend from her Farmington school, Florence Learned. They stayed in Munich for three months at the home of the Countess von Platen, née Stephanie Hamilton. The party then traveled through Italy and into Switzerland, temporarily establishing themselves at St. Moritz where they hiked along Alpine trails. Returning to Germany, Hoffman hired a tutor to help her perfect her German and employed a Mr. Levy to give her voice lessons. Levy became interested in Hoffman's desire to learn music, and on the days she attended the opera, he arrived to play the evening's music so Hoffman and her friends might be familiar with the program.

A cable interrupted her stay. Hoffman's friend's father was dangerously ill. They left Munich immediately for France. En route to Paris, Hoffman decided to shed the mourning clothes she had donned for her deceased grandfather. She telegraphed to alert a Parisian salon to expect her for fittings and to prepare workrooms to make the gowns she would need within forty-eight hours. Hoffman arrived in Paris on a Wednesday, and the salon furnished her with fourteen gowns of every imaginable description and for every occasion. The gowns were each tried on twice, packed, and placed on the train by Friday.[15] The party then crossed the English Channel, took a train to Liverpool, and boarded the ship for home.

On a subsequent European visit, Hoffman traveled with a Madame de Hegermann-Lindencrone to Germany "where it was understood that we would enter the family of Baroness v. Munchausen, a direct descendant of the famous traveler, whose son had married a friend of my aunt, Annette Estep."[16] In England, Hoffman was presented to Queen Victoria as well as the monarchs presiding over Sweden and Italy. Her favorite capital cities were Stockholm, clean and bright in the Scandinavian summer-time and Paris, the hub of European culture. At one cotillion in Stockholm, she was pleased when Prince Eugen, representative of the royal family, gave her his flag, indicative of being asked for a dance. He had to wait his turn, however, until she completed a dance with another partner who had done the same. Hoffman wrote, "That night at the Amaranthe was the first time in my life that I actually danced my slippers full of holes. I had heard of such an experience, but had no practical acquaintance with it."[17]

Hoffman returned to the United States in the mid-1890s and decided to rent a small cottage in Southampton, Massachusetts. She refurnished her new home to make it more comfortable and attractive. She borrowed horses and a phaeton from her aunt for her frequent trips to town. Hoffman noted:

> the house was in perfect order, the floors stained & waxed, the rugs put down, & in fact it was transformed. The house was too small to accommodate more than whoever happened to be chaperoning me at the moment, my two maids, & one suitor, but lunch was a free for all and there was quite a large choice [of beverages], although hard liquor was not encouraged.[18]

Hoffman loved horseback riding. She recalled: "When I was six . . . I rode a horse harnessed to the plow in Ohio, accoutered in an old lilac calico skirt, belonging to an aunt."[19] Although as a child Hoffman had broken her hip in a fall from a horse, she continued to enjoy horseback riding with her frequent guests at her Southampton home. She had six riding accidents in one month. Once, her horse, tripped by a wire, stepped full upon her face with its forefoot. Her sister, arriving at the scene, told her she must see a doctor. The doctor explained that he must take a few stitches. She answered, "Not on your life. . . . I have suffered all I am going to."[20] He said nothing further, but handed her a mirror. She gave one glance at herself, and holding firmly unto the arms of her chair, told him to go ahead.[21]

Hoffman returned to Europe frequently. She spent a considerable amount of time in Stockholm, attending concerts, dinners, cotillions, and mingling with the American rich and European royalty and aristocracy. In Paris, she kept racehorses that wore the same colors as her racing clothes—a white jacket, emerald sleeves, and a black velvet cap. Along with other members of the leisure class, Hoffman attended races at Chantilly, Longchamps, and the Grand Prix. She would not allow her horses to run in steeplechases, because she had witnessed several horses break their legs while jumping. In 1908 she was delighted when her horse, Flush Royal, beat two Vanderbilt horses at the Grand Prix.

Even in this ritualized society, Hoffman retained her sense of individuality. Due to the carelessness of a trainer, Flush Royal was killed in an unfortunate accident with another horse during practice runs. Her legal advisor at the time informed her that to collect the insurance on the horse, she would have to allow the insurance company to sue the other horse's owner. Never one to care about others' opinions of her actions, she put a notice of the insurance company's intention to sue in the newspaper whereupon she noted:

> the whole racing world was wrought up to an unbelievable pitch. Every one was looking down their noses at me and saying that it would be the death blow to all small owners. . . . I endured this attitude of the public as long as I had to, and then the Court proclaimed that the Insurance Co hadn't a leg to stand on and at once I became a public benefactor. The question had never come up before, and therefore an entirely new statute had been added to the existing list, and I was the instigator.[22]

Hoffman remained in Paris from 1900 to 1910. In that year, immediately before the finalization of her divorce, she decided to again return to America with her visiting grandmother and sister. Hoffman spent two comfortable years at the Hotel Gotham in New York City. In 1912, her niece, Eleanor Roosevelt, left California with her husband, Theodore Roosevelt Jr., and a new baby to make her home in New York City.[23] Hoffman loved her only niece and noted that "her husband's resources did not permit him to establish himself in a manner which I felt was due to my father and grandfather. . . . When I learned what house Mrs. Roosevelt had chosen, I cast about to find some means of avoiding the necessity of bringing up precious and highly-strung children in the vicinity of the Third Avenue elevated railroad." She decided to buy a house in New York City, which she could give to Eleanor. She had entered into real estate.

Hoffman bought a building at 17 East 54th Street for the purpose of giving it to her niece, making a $5,000 deposit on the full price of $150,000. She found that personal and financial problems in France, however, made it impossible to make a gift of the penthouse apartment. Instead, she furnished it for herself when she was in New York and rented it when she stayed in Paris. She frequented auction houses for furnishings and gloated over her bargains. For years, this building brought Hoffman nothing but problems. It had two mortgages on it for more money than she had paid (she failed to get a third). Hoffman also bought a penthouse apartment at 419 E. 57th Street and buildings at 1006 Fifth Avenue and 25-27 W. 56th Street. Hoffman's purchases were not confined to New York City; she bought Horse Island off Greenwich, Connecticut, and several lots in Jamaica.[24] In 1920, Hoffman sold the East Orange house that had belonged to her father for $30,250.[25]

In the 1920s, a tenant of the building at 17 East 54th Street, Emil Fraad, subleased the building to several tenants: Lily & Suzanne, Inc.; William Dutka; Peggy Hoyt, Inc.; and 17 East 54th Street Corporation. According to Hoffman, Fraad, "through a clever manipulation . . . sold his lease in such a manner as to seem a sublease."[26] Resenting his income from her building, Hoffman sued Fraad. Thus, she had entered not only the world of real estate, but the world of legal contest as well.[27] She remained in this legal world of powerful and influential men for the rest of her life.

Hoffman continually neglected the building. A tenant, William Dutka, a ladies' tailor and furrier, addressed a letter to Hoffman November 19, 1929 which read:

> The service in this building is perfectly disgusting. The elevator is always out of order. Just at present there are no lights. . . . How in the world do you expect my customers to come into my place, when two of my customers have phoned me, that they were down stairs, but due to no elevator and no lights they could not walk up. That was loss of sales. . . . Immediate attention is requested or I will hold you people reliable for the hindrance this is causing me.[28]

Dutka finally moved his business. Although Hoffman's attorneys addressed letters to the tenants warning them not to pay rent to Fraad, the court allowed him, rather than Hoffman, to collect rent during the eight-year period that the case was argued. The court restricted Hoffman herself from living in the building, which compelled her to find another home. She rented a small apartment on the top floor at 25 West 56th Street for eight years. She wrote William Kingsley, president of the United States Trust Company of New York:

> By the time you read as far as this you will feel like putting an icebag on your head, and I am terribly sorry to worry you with what must seem remote and intangible.
>
> I am not accustomed to be taken care of and it never occurs to me to feel deserted or lonely, but I can imagine tonight what joy some women must experience who have a strong right arm to cling to.[29]

Hoffman, forced to remove her furnishings from the 54th Street apartment, had them stored at the Atlas Storage Company, New York. The company mailed bill after bill to Hoffman which she neglected to pay. A beautiful Steinway grand piano was damaged by humidity in the storehouse. On one of Hoffman's visits to New York, she brought suit against the storage company, demanding they arrange to have the piano repaired. The storage company paid for the restoration of the piano, but Hoffman left it there for several more years, until it made its final move to North Carolina. Likewise, she failed to pay others for their services. Ida H. Buck, cleaning woman for her father, who managed the leasing of Hoffman's building, wrote:

> Dear Mrs. Hoffman! I would not ask you for a little check, but to save my old father from bankruptcy i [*sic*] am forced to do so. On account that your apartment was on the market for rent, it had to be kept in a good condition, as Mr. Buck will not show a dusty place. Going up there every day i [*sic*] dont [*sic*] think it will be to much asking $20 - a month. So please dear Madam i [*sic*] would be much obliged if you could help me out. Thanking you in advance for your kindness. With best regards.[30]

Throughout her lifetime, Hoffman continued this neglect of the settlement of her accounts. She exhibited this cavalier attitude toward members of all social levels. At the close of the legal battle with Fraad, Hoffman accused her attorney and friend, Herbert Satterlee, of negligence and charging exorbitant fees. Hoffman wrote:

> I should be very much surprised if [mistaken], for my memory of the items you enumerate is that I paid that bill in quite a different manner, & with much satisfaction, for I thought that the charge for all the negotiations connected with the purchase of this property, including the escrow which stretched over a period of eight years, was more than reasonable. I distinctly remember the circumstances, & when I made the final payment . . . I had the pleasure of handing Mr. Frederick a token of my appreciation, which while not sumptuous, was never-the-less sufficient to mark my sense of obligation.[31]

Satterlee, whose correspondence with Hoffman usually showed patience and courtesy, replied:

> Every time that I have taken up your letter . . . with the idea of answering it, I have put it down with the feeling that it would be kinder not to do so. I must, however, in justice to my partners and our whole office staff, resent your statement that there has been the greatest negligence in looking after your affairs. . . .
>
> Frankly, I do not enjoy being found fault with or having my office found fault with all the time. We won your litigation and got you back your house; we got the $24,000 for you that you wanted without your having to pay any commission or paying us anything for the service; we have carried your litigation for a long while and have never heard any suggestion from you that in any of your plans for financing or otherwise, we should receive any remuneration, except that we were to get the defendant to pay a bonus to cover it! How can [we] estimate the value of the services until we know how long they may have to continue or what they may involve?[32]

Several reasons for her parsimony stand out. Hoffman, afraid of being cheated, argued with attorneys, bankers, book dealers, servants, and others over their service fees. She refused to understand that other persons set their own pay scales and that she could not pay them only what she thought they deserved. She frequently misunderstood providers, bound instead to her own opinion. Also, when absorbed in one problem, Hoffman frequently allowed other considerations to remain unresolved. Surprisingly, given her inheritances, Hoffman often lamented that she had no cash available and gave it as a reason for her failure to pay debts.[33] This never stopped her, however, from ordering on credit those things she wanted. Exasperation and resentment filled many letters addressed to her from those she owed money.

As far as the Fraad lawsuit, the court finally rendered a verdict based on an old law that forbade subleasing. She never received the money owed her, however, for Fraad declared bankruptcy. Hoffman could not make mortgage payments, and in the early 1930s, she lost the East 54th Street building for nonpayment of the mortgage.[34] She also lost the East 57th Street penthouse for failure to pay an electric bill, although she contended that "the hall light must have been nefariously switched onto my current."[35] By 1936, Hoffman had either lost or sold her properties in New York City, Connecticut, and Jamaica.

Acquisition of property in New York was not Hoffman's only interest. Enfranchised at the age of fifty-eight, Hoffman had for many years belonged to her aunt's organization to educate women politically, financially supporting lectures and providing literature. She was affiliated with the Republican Committee of 100 and contributed to a fund to build the New York City town hall. Although she did not write often concerning politics in America (she spent so much of her time in France), her politics reflected her class. Hoffman commented during the Depression that she thought the country's economic problems were caused by buying on the installment plan, labor unions, and the end of the gold standard. A staunch Republican, she mistakenly predicted in 1933 that Congress would impeach President Franklin D. Roosevelt before his term ended.

Seeking social change as well as political change, women at this time overturned conventional customs of feminine dress. Hoffman, and thousands of other women, began to wear pants. She ordered various materials and had her dressmaker sew several pairs of trousers for her to wear while working and exercising out-of-doors. Hoffman's housekeeper, Maggie, wrote to her and confessed:

> let me tell you that you are not the only one that wears breeches . . . I donned the boots and breeches too. I felt rather out of place when I first made my public appearance as I had never worn them in my life and of course they all laughed at me and Sam [her husband] said, 'You will have a pipe or a can of snuff next,' but they are so much more comfortable to work outside in than dresses and [I] have ordered rubber boots so that the wet weather won't keep me in.[36]

Hoffman, in spite of the stocks and bonds inherited from her grandfather's and father's estates and her various properties and buildings, continued in financial difficulty. Storage companies, insurance companies, attorneys, brokers, stores, jewelers, property managers, and servants mailed frequent letters requesting payment. Often she either replied with complaints of services and fees or ignored the letters. Lester D. Egbert, an agent of Brown, Crosby & Co., Inc. wrote, "Just as the sun rises every morning, so I show up on the horizon the tenth of each month to present my insurance bills."[37]

Hoffman, apparently, did not allow debts to interfere with her style of living. Years later, she typed in her autobiography:

> Although, when he wrote 'Chips of Jade,' Arthur Guiterman had never met me, I have always felt that my aura must have inspired the following lines:
>
> Not a penny to her name,
> Runs to market just the same.
>
> for it so exactly describes me. I have never had the money in hand to do any of the things which I eventually accomplished. And as I write I don't actually know what I have accomplished.[38]

Perhaps owing to her privileged place in society, no one initially refused her goods or services. Although she owed them, merchants usually sent her requests. A good example is a letter she wrote to a publishing company:

> Dear Mr. Lauriat, I have received your bill this morning, and I shall ask you to extend your usual leniency in the matter of payment . . . It will not be necessary to remind me as fortunately I have not got very many bills. I would like to have you send me a copy of: *Released for Publication, History of Pirates, Lawrence and the Arabian Adventures, Cranford, The Adventures of an African Slaver. . .*
>
> Thanking you and your prompt attention to my requirements.[39]

Lauriet's company delivered the books, then mailed bill after bill after bill.

Besides her frequent Atlantic crossings to Europe, Hoffman traversed the Pacific. In 1925 Hoffman spent the winter in China as the guest of the British minister to China, Sir Ronald Macleay and his wife, Evelyn. This was the same year that Sun Yat-sen, leader of the Chinese Nationalist Party, died. Sun Yat-sen and his followers sought to free China from outside influences. After his death, his successor, Chiang Kai-shek, waged war against warlords in northern China in hopes of uniting the country. Hoffman noted: "Entering China was one of the most informal things I ever saw. We simply walked off of the boat, without incurring the smallest hindrance."[40] As they traveled to Peking, their train moved aside numerous times to allow troop trains to pass "with unfortunate soldiers packed like herrings on flat cars evidently going to the front."[41] Returning soldiers filled Hoffman's car, lying several deep on the floor, but this did not "prevent Kaufmann [the Danish minister] from procuring a perfectly adequate lunch, from no one knew where."[42] In China, her maid, Charlotte, ate at the same table, "as no white person is ever required to eat with the house staff in an Oriental establishment."[43]

Hoffman carried her gaily colored parrot, Polly, on her travels to China and nothing would induce her to allow Polly to travel in the baggage car. She enlisted the help of a small boy to smuggle the bird aboard. After receiving his tip, the youngster fled to tell the authorities, whereupon Hoffman hid the caged bird in a corner built for the conductor, "assuming [a] most innocent & stupid expression"[44] when officials appeared and inquired for the bird. Hoffman, unable to answer their questions in Chinese, appeared unconcerned, and the men retired, warning the boy not to disturb them again with false information. As soon as Hoffman removed Polly from her hiding place, the parrot "entertained the whole car with her witty comments on the trip."[45]

Reflecting her sense of priorities, Hoffman recounted the "most harrowing experience of [her] trip."[46] Needing to wash her hair after four weeks at sea, she discovered that the water was so hard no amount of rinsing would remove the soap! Added to this, the electric current burned out her hair-dryer. She learned to have distilled water on hand for hair washing.

Hoffman enjoyed her winter in China so thoroughly that she considered establishing a residence in Peking. Years later, she recounted delightful rides in a rickshaw. Kept warm wrapped in a coat of black brocade "lined with wild cats with their tails left on," Hoffman rode through the streets surrounded by "stars in the clear windless nights that seemed so close in the cloudless sky one felt that one could almost pick them out of the heavens."[47]

In 1930 Hoffman entrained to Florida with a friend and sailed to Puerto Rico to visit her niece, Eleanor, when Theodore Roosevelt. Jr. was civil governor there. She also visited Eleanor in the Philippines during his governorship in those islands in 1932.[48]

Certainly, the Depression increased Hoffman's economic difficulties. She failed to collect rent from several of her tenants during these years, finally taking three to court for rent recovery. Similarly, her investments in railroads and surface roads returned increasingly smaller dividends. Moreover, Williamson Pell, first vice-president of the United States Trust Company, reported: "All the mills, with the exception of Spartan Mills, have suspended dividend payments. Your income is less than $200 and we are beginning proceedings to sell your stocks."[49]

Yet, Hoffman continued her many activities. Throughout the late 1920s and early 1930s, Hoffman spent many summer days in Canada with friends. Passing through Montreal, Ottawa, and Mattewa, they arrived at a lodge in Kippewa, Quebec, on Kippewa Lake. The hunting camp measured three hundred square miles with a house located on a fifty acre island on the lake. Located on the first floor was a huge sitting room with window-lined walls and a floor covered with the hides of various types of bear, shot by the owner or his guests. Guests usually filled the many rooms, and in the evenings they played round card games. Hoffman rose in the mornings before the other guests to get in and out of the bathroom, which was heated with a roaring fire and complete with white enamel fittings.

During the day, while the men were away hunting or fishing, Hoffman worked out-of-doors, chopping trees for firewood. Although her host furnished her with a hatchet, Hoffman soon outgrew it and used a large axe without his knowledge. She found her "sense of beauty offended by the dead branches which were killed by the snow on the under part of the fir trees."[50] Using all her skill and strength, she would climb up to knock off these branches with a tap from the back of the axe. Later she wrote:

> I was balanced on top of a pile of fallen trees one day in a most precarious position, when the whole mass changed, and my heavy axe came down within a hair's breadth of the big vein in my wrist. It took some planning to conceal this small cut, which I did not dare dress in any way for fear of attracting attention to my carelessness and thereby curtailing my happiness in my occupation. I occasionally look at the scar and thank my stars that I still retained hold of the axe handle and saved a worse wound.[51]

Hoffman devised an apron with a strap around the neck and loops on the opposite corners, which enabled her to carry a heavier load of wood than if she was using only her arms. She carried the logs to the pathway and piled them, ready to be hauled to the woodshed. As she worked, wild animals visited without any thought of danger. She especially loved the ermine, "regal in their whole attitude."[52] Hoffman decided that without a doubt, they deserved to be "chosen to deck Royalty."[53]

While the other guests hunted, boated, fished, or played cards, Hoffman made paths around the house of boulders nearby which were split like pieces of slate. After digging under the large rocks, she would fit a strong pine underneath and pry it loose by bouncing up and down on the other end of the sapling. She wrote that she "felt as an inventor must whose machine consents to work for the first time."[54] Her host did not want the guides continually fatigued in helping Hoffman, as he had engaged them only for hunting and fishing, so Hoffman made the pathways alone, laying them along the pine-needle covered ground in permanent positions.

Apparently during these summer excursions, Hoffman first desired a large estate. She noted, "After I had spent seven hours a day for several years in beautifying some one else's property it occurred to me that it might be a good plan to have one of my own."[55] As she began a search for an expanse of property, circumstances in France led to her first purchase of a country place.

In 1892, Hoffman had leased a house in Paris to provide a centrally located home for her frequent European visits, but in 1895 she made a more permanent move to France from New York, taking all her belongings. Until 1922, Hoffman lived in Paris with intervals in America. In that year, while Hoffman visited America, the owner of her Parisian home, Baroness Willy de Rothschild of Germany requested her to find another house as she needed it for her grown children. Hoffman sailed to France to oversee the packing of her belongings; she had lived in the house for twenty-seven years. During World War I, her niece, Eleanor, had stayed in the house while her husband, Col. Theodore Roosevelt Jr. was at the front.

After searching the city for houses to let, Hoffman heard of an attractive place in the country near Paris. It was extraordinarily reasonable, as it lay in a military zone and had been "disaffected owing to long distance fire."[56] Upon visiting it, Hoffman thought the house too small but decided it could be enlarged. The estate consisted of twelve and one-half acres with carefully groomed lawns and well-tended gardens. After a few preliminaries, she bought the Chateau des Landes in Suresnes, "a name only and not a Chateau, as that had been destroyed during the Franco-Prussian war."[57] Hoffman attained her goal to own land and moved her belongings into her new home.

Although she had hoped to establish permanent residence in France, she learned that the French government, the Front Populaire, needed a portion of her property for the widening of a boulevard. This roadway would reduce her property by approximately one acre. Hoffman speculated that the government's action would also lower the land's monetary value, hence she sought a buyer. Although she failed to find a purchaser for the property, Hoffman refused the government's offer of two hundred thousand francs. She thought that the government was taking advantage of her as a woman and an American.[58] Informing one of her financial advisors of the problem, Hoffman declared, "I don't mean to convey that it would be desirable to take it for granted that all women or even a few women or even any women know what they are about as well as I do, but it would be helpful if it were possible to discriminate," and added that "one of the favorite singers of the Opera, obtained one million francs for her one [acre]."[59] Hoffman decided to take the French government to court. At first she claimed that she "had the wonderful luck to discover a most unusual lawyer, of the old school, & he took care of my claim with vigour & ability."[60]

Before the court decided the case, however, events in New York necessitated her return to America. Upon sailing, her "vigorous" and "able" attorney advised her to take what the government offered, as it would not be tied by a court's decision.

In 1933, back in New York City, Hoffman chose a different maneuver to get her price from the French government. She considered herself, unfortunately it seems, equal to any man in legal capability and, in one letter, even asked her New York attorney: "Don't you think it a pity I was not a lawyer?"[61] Hoffman wrote a letter to her niece, Eleanor, explaining the property situation to her. She warned Eleanor that, as her heir, the controversy involved her, as the widened boulevard would cause a decrease in the estate's value. Hoffman urged Eleanor, who was in France at the time, to meet with the mayor of Suresnes. She told Eleanor that "with your personality and charm he could be induced to offer a trifle more than he has."[62] Continuing, Hoffman advised her to "send for Augusta and the papers which are the plans for the proposed change. You will quickly understand what it is all about . . . The crux of the matter is that after I had signed them they came back and requested me to concede further ground which I refused to do."[63] Hoffman confided to Eleanor:

> the reason for the mayor's low offer is because I asked him if he could negotiate a loan which need not be recorded in the books in the nature of a mortgage in order to avoid drawing the attention of the taxes assessors to the value of the property. My income tax last year was less than 10 dollars! And he advised this manner of conferring a mutual benefit.[64]

Through Eleanor, Hoffman determined to obtain more money for her property. Ending the letter, Hoffman advised: "If you would like to take the time to give a party in Suresnes in connection with seeing the authorities it would be nice to ask your guests to lunch . . . and I think it would be a very unusual opportunity to put yourself on the map as the future owner of something unique, and you can be certain that you will not only have good food but good wine. I do not need to tell you this."[65]

Hoffman assured Eleanor that it would be of vital importance to both of them in the future and that the money would be a "God-send" to her in the present.

It seems that Eleanor did not do as Hoffman asked or did not succeed; the French government decided to seize Hoffman's entire estate. Hoffman contended that the French had no right to any of her property, as she intended it as a memorial to Eleanor's brother-in-law Quentin Roosevelt, an American aviator killed in France July 14, 1918 in a dogfight with a German pilot and buried at Chammery.

Claiming she lacked available cash, Hoffman eventually became desperate. She needed money for her lawsuit and apparently had other financial difficulties in Paris as well. Hoffman wrote her New York attorney that she hoped to meet with her trustees, "which will relieve the tension of the financial situation concerning my arrears in this city."[66]

Answering her plea for money, however, the president of the United States Trust Company on Wall Street replied: "I am sorry to say that we cannot loan you any more money. Please do not ask me again as it is so embarrassing to say no to you."[67] She pawned her collection of laces, but got only $240 for it. One of her New York attorneys joked: "By the way, did you ever go down to Monte Carlo? I cross my fingers with the hope that you would break the bank, and then our troubles would soon disappear."[68] Hoffman did indeed visit the casinos there often and worked on various schemes to "break the bank," especially at roulette.

Hoffman's troubles refused to disappear. The struggle for her Parisian estate continued for many years. Finally, a short time before July 28, 1938, the French government confiscated her entire Suresnes estate. On that date, Hoffman wrote a letter stating that it was her ambition to have the "present decree annulled and to offer at the current market value a portion of the Chateau which is not indispensable from it, to the authorities, upon condition that I retain the balance."[69]

Hoffman ultimately lost her French home, which grew in her memory to become "the most beautiful estate in the entire countryside."[70] According to her, she sailed for the United States in 1938 due to the "disgraceful behaviour of the Nazi Govt,"[71] rather than the loss of her estate. She never returned to Europe.

Failed in her ambition to secure a country estate in France, Hoffman returned to property she had purchased in 1917, her only remaining home. It consisted of half of the island of Bogue Banks in North Carolina. During the years 1917 through 1934, Hoffman made sporadic trips to Bogue Banks. Characteristically, Hoffman neglected this property whenever absent but she had at certain times attempted to manage her North Carolina property through a series of overseers. When she frequented Bogue Banks, friends and relatives visited, but found the island alien, primitive, and uncomfortable. A friend wrote of Hoffman's North Carolina home:

> Abounding in beauties of nature
> This island's inhabited too,
> Wild boar, cattle-ticks, red-bugs & serpents,
> Thrive, as not many living things do![72]

Hoffman contrastingly portrayed it: "Nothing can ever describe the wonderful feeling of the summer air when driving on the Beach. It is actually caressing, and seems palpably to envelop one and the wonder of the moonlight has sometimes kept my eyes open through the whole night."[73]

Assuredly, Hoffman enjoyed her inherited wealth during her younger years. She filled her life with travel, gambling, entertaining, and shopping. At the age of fifty, however, which corresponded with the marriage of her only niece, Eleanor, to Theodore Roosevelt, Jr., Hoffman decided to invest her money in property, with disastrous results.

Hoffman had initially purchased New York City property to provide a home for Eleanor, Theodore, and their child. It would appear that Hoffman, after Eleanor's entry into the prominent Roosevelt family, finally saw an opening into the top echelon of New York society. With Eleanor's motherhood, Hoffman also found future inheritors of her wealth.

Chapter Two

Bogue Banks

ogue Banks, protected by Core Banks and Cape Lookout from the destruction of storms called "nor'easters," produced large dense stands of maritime forest. The largest trees, live oak, white oak, holly, and cedar, grow close to the ocean. Subject to constant salt-laden winds, these trees form a meshwork of tightly interwoven, gnarled forms, bent along the direction of the prevailing southwesterly winds. Nearer the beach, between the primary and secondary dunes, smaller plants and shrubs such as morning glory, pennywort, smilax vine, and wax myrtle anchor the soil against the wind. Along the sound side of the island, protected from the salt spray, pine trees, sea elder, Virginia Creeper, and grape vines meet the marsh grasses.

The wildlife is varied and plentiful on the island. Deer, foxes, raccoons, opossums, lizards, and snakes are the largest animals on the banks. Herons, egrets, and ibises wade slowly through the marshes, looking for fish. Ospreys and brown pelicans dive for food in the waters, while seagulls and terns wheel overhead. Cormorants sit on pilings, spreading their wings to dry. Songbirds fill the trees. Insects are abundant. In the summer, the sound of cicadas is overpowering. The maritime forest protects the barrier island from the devastating effects of coastal storms. Now reduced considerably by development, this splendid maritime forest covered Bogue Banks in Hoffman's time.

Early in 1915, Hoffman, while reading the *New York Herald* one morning in her New York City apartment, noticed the following advertisement:

A PARADISE OF A HOME

FOR SALE THREE MILES FROM BEAUFORT, N.C.

LATELY BUILT FOR PRIVATE USE, FOURTEEN

BEDROOMS, THREE BATHS STEAM HEAT, ELEC

TRICITY; FURNISHED OR UNFURNISHED; LARGE

FIG ORCHARD AND OTHER FRUITS; 40 ACRES OR
160; 120 ACRES PINES; FINE FOR HUNT CLUB
OR SANATORIUM; FISHING, DUCK SHOOTING;
LIVING FROM OWN BEACH; OYSTERS, CLAMS,
CRABS, SHRIMP, SCALLOPS TURTLE; PERFECT
CLIMATE; NO MALARIA, NO SNOW; NEARER GULF
STREAM THAN ANY POINT ABOVE FLORIDA.
BORDEN, 523 FIFTH AVENUE.[74]

Considering her resolve to own a piece of wild land, made on earlier vacations to the Canadian wilderness, Hoffman called Borden and found that he was the son-in-law of the property's owner, Mrs. Gilman Perkins of Rochester, New York. By lunchtime, an enthused Hoffman had written to her for the particulars of the property. The two women exchanged letters for several weeks, with a final agreement that Hoffman should visit Mrs. Perkins on her next visit to her vacation home in Beaufort.

Several weeks later in May 1915, Hoffman departed by train from New York to travel to North Carolina.[75] She must have felt increasingly a stranger in a strange land as she traveled to Carteret County on the Atlantic coast. The South had developed into a much different world than the North. Slow-paced in comparison to the busy and bustling Northerners, Southerners may have "failed to develop the institutions their northern neighbors had, [however] they had more or less freely chosen to follow the way of life others condemned.[76] They "regard[ed] the Southern way of life as superior to that of New England," assuming that the "first end of life is living itself."[77] Of the Tar Heel state, Walter Hines Page, a North Carolinian removed to New York, wrote: "The world must have some corner in it where men sleep and sleep and dream and dream, and North Carolina is as good a spot for that as any."[78]

In the rural, poor eastern North Carolina counties, Carteret County numbered among the poorest, the people there dependent upon farming and fishing for a living. Their educational system hardly existed. Although the state's government made advances in expenditures on education, increasing from $950,317 in 1900 to $4,067,793 in 1913, North Carolina's "public-education system . . . still remained far below the national average at the end of this period."[79] In Carteret County, during the years 1903-1921, "teachers' salaries were distressingly low, ranging from $18.00 to $85.00 per month, depending on the area served. In addition, [teachers] were subjected to dismissal for religious beliefs. Their contract also called for extra curricular work in churches and Sunday Schools."[80] During this period, the length of the school term was extended to four months.[81]

On her journey, before switching trains in Goldsboro, North Carolina, Hoffman left her sleeping car for the dining car to find milk for her coffee. The train stopped, and she paid no attention when it started again. A few moments later the conductor came through, asking for tickets, and discovered she was on the wrong train. The engineer stopped the train and Hoffman later recalled:

> They put me out among some cotton fields, out of sight of Goldsboro, and naturally before I had had a chance to swallow the ever too hot coffee. I was really nonplused. There I was without any blouse under my cape, no hat, no gloves, and no breakfast.[82]

Hoffman asked an "old darkey" walking in the opposite direction if he thought she could still catch the train. He nonchalantly replied, "Oh, she gone, some time back." Hoffman trudged the distance to Goldsboro only to find the train at the station. When her absence on the train had been discovered, the engineer reversed direction, and the train waited for her. Hoffman wrote that "no Cinderella, with a golden coach was ever more delighted than I was, and I finally got my breakfast at the next change three hours farther on."[83]

Hoffman, accustomed to the fashionable worlds of New York and Paris, was shocked when, stopping for the night at a lodging in North Carolina, she found a cockroach in her room "literally as big as a mouse." Later, she recalled:

> at my behest a [servant] spent the better part of fifteen minutes on his hands & knees armed with my umbrella poking it out from its various retreats under the furniture. He finally dispatched it but left it where it fell, which made me feel that I was spending the night with a corpse, & decided me to forego any thought of going to bed or taking a bath,

> so I put on my wrapper & lay on top of the bed to be prepared to leap in case of necessity.[84]

Hoffman arrived in Beaufort and after several days of consideration decided that the Perkins property was unsuitable, as it was too large a house on too small a lot. She stayed on for a few more days, however, as she delighted in the warm spring weather of the Southern east coast and enjoyed the town of Beaufort, located on the mainland, with Core Banks, Cape Lookout, and Shackleford Banks nearby.

Beaufort, founded in 1709, possessed many well-preserved homes from that century. In colonial days, the small port had become a favorite hiding place for pirates. Edward Teach, or Blackbeard, owned a house in Beaufort and stopped there often to visit his wife. In the 1860s, the Civil War interrupted a period of prosperity in Beaufort. On April 14, 1861 a Confederate force under Captain Josiah Pender took command of Fort Macon, which guarded the town. Three Union brigades under General Ambrose E. Burnside captured Beaufort on March 26, 1862. It remained in Union hands until the end of the war.[85]

In 1915 Beaufort remained small, isolated, and oriented to the sea. When Hoffman decided to return to New York, a visiting member of Perkins's family told Hoffman one day that she must not leave North Carolina without seeing the island called, by its owner, the Isle of Pines. Hoffman asked if it would be possible to visit it. Perkins obtained a boat and took the household over. Hoffman noted, "It was very good of [Perkins], for she hated the water, and went only to give me pleasure. I had no sooner put my foot on land than I decided that I must own that divine spot."[86] Hoffman found a small frame house sitting on a knoll overlooking Bogue Sound. The house, surrounded by a thick forest of pine, holly, bay, live oak, and dogwood, needed repair. The property stretched the width of the island, from sound to ocean, and measured approximately thirteen miles long, roughly half the entire island. The owner, John A. Royall, a native of Massachusetts who seldom visited, and the people who lived in Salter Path, a small fishing village about six miles west of the Royall house, comprised its only inhabitants.

Hoffman spent several more days at Perkins's Beaufort home. Extremely interested in the island property, Hoffman asked Perkins to invite Royall and his wife to lunch, as they were then visiting their island home. To her disappointment, Royall did not come, but she did obtain from Royall's wife an invitation for lunch and a walk through the woods and over to the beach.

Hoffman visited the Royalls several times and arranged to rent a small cottage near their house, which had been built for Royall's physician. Over the next two years, Hoffman spent much time on Bogue Banks and developed an irresistible desire to transform the property into a personal estate.

Although Hoffman expressed her wish to Royall to buy his property, they could not agree on a price and Royall did not appear interested in selling the land. By 1917, however, the situation had changed. According to Hoffman, one day as she and Royall sat on the porch of her cottage, he asked her to make him an offer on the property. Although Hoffman informed him that she could not possibly pay the price he had asked, Royall bid her again to name a price. Hoffman replied "$40,000 for your holdings," whereupon Royall countered, "Could you make it $45,000?" Hoffman later wrote:

> I was so afraid that he would see the joy in my eyes that I kept them on my lap, while I pondered this possibility. Finally I said, "Well I might." whereupon he got up & said: "I think I must talk it over with my wife." "Not at all," I replied, "come right in here & sign the contract," which he did & went upon his way.[87]

After the official transferal of the deed on September 11, 1917, Hoffman later recalled:

> There was a little clearing on the road to the beach which had a group of longleaf pines which I had always looked on longingly, knowing as I did how much they would be improved by having more air & light, & the first thing I did to celebrate my victory was to take my axe & go & chop down every encroaching tree, & throw them all down behind the ravine, where the depredation would not be noticed. I had one of the supreme moments of my life, & could not describe the thrill of possession of one of the most beautiful spots still in existence.[88]

Hoffman's attorney, John H. Judge of New York City, confirmed the transaction through his law firm on July 21, 1917. The title was for the sale of the Glover tract, with an additional adjacent tract bought on July 30, 1917 called the Thomas tract, which included a small fishing village. Included was an option to buy two other adjacent tracts: the Johnson tract, located to the east of the property, and the remaining western end of the banks. Hoffman thought that Royall asked more for the Johnson tract than it was worth, so she contacted S.P. Hancock, sheriff and tax collector of Carteret County, who looked into the matter for her. Hancock contacted the firm of Thompson & Smathers, court appointed guardians of the tract's owner, John Johnson, who had been declared insane. Subsequently, Hancock wrote Hoffman that she could obtain the entire three hundred acre tract of land for $4,000, provided the sale remained secret. Hancock warned, "you know as well as I do that if these people found out that a wealthy woman wants to buy [the property] what a difficult thing it would be to purchase [it] at anything like reasonable figures."[89] Hoffman, through Hancock, received a quitclaim deed for the Johnson property. A few years later Hoffman also purchased another tract called the Classy Carter property, which consisted of three hundred sixty acres of thickly wooded land on the mainland across from the island.

Hoffman began to spend some time in her new home in the South, but favored New York City and Paris. She moved into the Royall house, which she named Shore House, and wrote: "It was a wonderful place at the time, one of the last remaining retreats, isolated from all the world & its fripperies. No telephone, electricity, radio, or noise, with the exception of the elements."[90]

Gradually, Hoffman began adding rooms onto her home until it became large and rambling, consisting of eighteen rooms, six bathrooms, and several basements. She referred to the basement under her bedroom as the "storm room." The only entrance to it was through Hoffman's private bathroom. She used that cellar during thunderstorms, which had terrified her from childhood. On the outside of the main structure, covered porches, verandas, and long decks surrounded the house. Local workers cleared a path to the beach until it was wide enough for an automobile. She "made history" one Saturday in driving "up the Beach & across the island." The men had laid some planks over the soft sand and in a "borrowed car, for the first time in eternity, an automobile crossed the wonderful pine forest."[91]

Transportation to the mainland was by boat. Hoffman had a dock built on the sound and purchased a motorboat which she named *Fred*. Although in the mid-1800s steam became a means of powering boats in Carteret County, sails still powered the boats of the fishermen at the small village on the banks called Salter Path.[92] According to Hoffman, who made little contact with the villagers, *Fred* proved a temptation to the Salter Path men, some of whom worked for her periodically. Hoffman related that one Saturday, three of the men assured her that they needed *Fred*. Hoffman later wrote that "the natives of this region are impelled by a force stronger than themselves to get to Morehead City on Saturday morning."[93] Although a stiff wind had begun, the men left for the mainland. One of their purchases was a coop of chickens that was left on the dock while they finished other tasks. By the time they were ready to leave, a gale had blown up, leaving all thought of returning that evening out of the question. Although the wind damaged other boats in the harbor, the villagers were obligated to hold *Fred* off the sea wall with poles. Hoffman later recalled:

> It must have been an arduous piece of work. In commenting on it to me later, dear old Cooper Adams, the one reliable inhabitant of Salter Path, said: "I reckon Bert's chickens must have fared mighty common!" I never think of those unfortunate fowl, out all night in a howling rain & wind without thinking of Cooper's remark.[94]

Hoffman cleared away shrubs and trees as she had in Canada. In the front of the house, she supervised the planting of a large, heartshaped garden. Possibly in the hope of creating gardens on the order of the great European estates, Hoffman also hired a brick mason to build a series of terraces sloping down to the sound for rose gardens. Hoffman loved roses and ordered several crates of different varieties from a supplier in Boston. The top terrace was planted with dark pink *Paul Neron*, which she had seen on a trip to Cuba. The next terrace was filled with lighter pink *Capitaine Christy*. Finally, on the third terrace grew *Frau Karl Druschki*. She and a companion took care of the roses the first season and had the satisfaction of cutting flowers that she thought were so enormous they seemed almost vulgar. Absent from Bogue Banks for long periods, she found her roses disappearing little by little, according to Hoffman, "due to ignorance, lack of obedience to her directions, and care."[95] She bemoaned the fact that she had never photographed her roses, believing them to be permanent.

Hoffman received visitors on the island. Sisters Grace and Alexandra made the trip by train. A cousin, Nancy, and an uncle, Henry M. Sanders visited. Her niece, Eleanor, came once, Hoffman recalled, by yacht with "old & intimate friends of her father-in-law."[96] Hoffman's attorneys, John H. Judge and Arthur H. Haaran, also visited the island. After cautioning her guests that there were no worldly diversions on the banks, they spent time relaxing, fishing, boating, and walking. Hoffman used a small, open pavilion of oriental design built on the sound for entertaining. She called it the Tea House. Visitors sat in the shade, enjoying the view of the mainland.

Hoffman soon learned that temperature and humidity in the South differed greatly from that in New York, Canada, or France. She ordered the shipment of the long-stored New York Steinway to her new home. She played the piano for several months until it became evident she would have to ship it back to New York. She had not reckoned with the high humidity. That, and the lack of trained personnel to service the instrument, soon caused it to become hopelessly out of tune. Hoffman, with her trained musician's ear, could not bear to hear the untuned piano.

Hoffman often cooked for her guests. She had learned the art of cooking in school and prided herself on her desserts. Often, when her niece Eleanor visited, Hoffman prepared all the food, in part because she had problems with her local cooks who did not follow her precise instructions. Once, upon first arriving at Shore House with a guest, she decided to make coffee. After roasting and grinding the coffee beans, she prepared the coffee and waited for her guest's "exclamations of surprise & delight."[97] The guest, however, formed an opinion that was not what she had expected. After tasting the horrible brew, Hoffman found the cause. The coffee grinder had hung on the wall since her last visit and what she had served was more than half rust.

On one occasion, Hoffman traveled to Bogue Banks on an unconventional mode of transportation. In 1933, at seventy years of age, feeling "unduly affluent and in a burst of enthusiasm,"[98] she bought a 1929 Indian three-wheeled motorcycle with a side-car from Nicolo Pisapia of Brooklyn, and with a companion, rode the motorcycle the entire trip, packed with luggage, which "did not prevent [them] from making 75 miles an hour all the way from Richmond to New Bern." [99]

As with her homes in New York City and Paris, Hoffman soon began having problems on her island home. A Northern woman with definite ideas about business and management, she valued efficiency, promptness, and hard work. As one historian, James C. Cobb, fittingly wrote:

> Enlightened northerners, if forced to live in the South, would insist on remaking their new home in the image of their old one. . . . The insistence of professional South-watchers that a more prosperous South must become a drawling version of the North resulted from a projection their own values and prejudices on a population . . . who apparently saw life somewhat differently.[100]

People in Carteret County changed little, preferring an easy pace of life marked more by the passing of tides and seasons than by dates and appointments. They made their living farming, growing cabbage, potatoes, and corn. A large menhaden industry flourished, which employed many local men. Individual fishermen caught fish, clams, oysters, scallops, and crabs.[101] Natives would not eat shrimp, but shipped them to New York, a market that brought them approximately four dollars for one hundred pounds of shrimp. Families would bring the shrimp from the boat, head them, wash them, and load them on a truck which carried them to a waiting train bound for New York.

For entertainment, people held outdoor dances, attended movies, or played baseball. Usually, they simply got together and talked on front porches. Attending church was an important and expected function. The majority of people in the county belonged to either the Methodist or Baptist church.[102]

A few local men worked during the summer season for the tourists that frequented Atlantic Beach, a "watering place" for the wealthy which developed on Bogue Banks immediately after Hoffman purchased her island property. In 1916, Von Bedsworth of Morehead City, purchased one hundred acres of property on Bogue Banks and, in 1918, built the Royal Pavilion, bathhouses, and a one-hundred-room hotel "which met with instant success."[103] In 1928, two corporations comprised of men from Morehead City and Beaufort financed the building of a wooden toll bridge from Morehead City to the new resort. The state bought the bridge in 1936 for approximately $50,000 and removed the tolls. On the beach, a dance hall and casino were built, and Atlantic Beach became "a most chic place to be."[104] Although a road existed on the island to the east from Atlantic Beach to Fort Macon, the village of Salter Path was accessible only by boat.

Hoffman disliked the new Atlantic Beach resort, which brought the "vacationing public accommodations directly on the beach"[105] and constantly complained about it to authorities. Although the property adjoined her land, Shore House actually was located several miles away. She had purchased her North Carolina property for quiet and seclusion from the rest of the world. Hoffman called the hotel and bathhouses a "blot upon her happiness" and a "great cross to [bear]." Delighted when the government condemned the buildings and offered them for sale, she decided to buy them for the lumber to continue building onto her home and also to erect a barn. Hoffman wrote, "Isn't it too wonderful? I just dislike a thing and it is removed. I am simply filled with wonder, love, and praise." [106]

Hoffman experienced continual problems with the mail service, which she considered haphazard and inefficient. She had an enormous amount of business to attend to while at Bogue Banks and demanded that the postal service deliver her mail promptly. She first received her mail from the mailboat that delivered to the residents at Salter Path. This arrangement clearly was unsatisfactory to her, for she soon asked her correspondents to address her mail to the Morehead City post office. Hoffman still had mail delivery problems, even from Morehead City, the county's largest town. Within a two week period, she complained: "Dear Miss Curtis . . . Did I tell you that as a last straw the P.M. is holding my mail in Morehead City on the days that the boat does not run? Did you ever?" "Dear Mr. Judge . . . this letter lay for 12 days in the P.O. in Morehead City." "Dear Mr. Bush . . . the P.O. has recently refused to deliver my mail except to the R.F.D. boat which comes over but three times a week so that it takes more than ten days before I can get an answer back to New York." "Dear Miss Curtis . . . it seems the mailboat has been sitting out on a shoal!"[107]

Hoffman made an application for her own post office, which was approved on July 12, 1919 as the Bogue Banks post office with Hoffman as its first and only postmaster.[108] Still, she did not get regular, daily postal service. The following year she appealed to North Carolina Senator Furnifold Simmons who inquired of the Postmaster General: "About a year ago there was established on the coast of North Carolina on an island, the post office of Bogue Banks with Mrs. Hoffman as Postmaster. This office would naturally be supplied . . . from Morehead City. There is, however, no route now supplying the post office."[109] Simmons requested an inspection of the problem. That summer, Hoffman commented on her incoming correspondence: "I live on a desert island and more time is consumed in reaching it after the letter has arrived from New York than it took on the way down."[110] On August 16, 1921 her frustration and anger are quite evident as she declared, "It is enough to induce me to blow up the P.O. at my next opportunity."[111]

Hoffman's correspondence revealed that, three years later, she had mail problems of a different kind. The postmaster at the village of Salter Path, Hettie Ann Willis, hospitalized for an operation, did not inform the United States Postal Service, and for some time, no one took care of the mail. Hoffman disparagingly commented: "This does not surprise me; knowing as I do that those unfortunate women cannot even tell the time I am quite of the opinion that it would be useless to expect them to keep post office books."[112] Finally, Harvey Willis of Salter Path wrote to the Postmaster General in Washington, DC, about the problem, and the Salter Path post office was discontinued for a three week period in January 1924.[113] During the period of discontinuation, the postal service delivered the Salter Path mail to Hoffman's post office at Shore House. The Salter Path people neglected or refused to pick up their mail there. It piled up considerably among Hoffman's own personal correspondence, driving her to distraction. Hoffman's Bogue Banks post office was disestablished on June 30, 1926. The post office at Salter Path continued to serve the residents.

In 1942, as World War II began for the United States, Hoffman remained at Shore House, as the financial future looked bleak and there she had no rent to pay. She later wrote:

> It is a solace in these days of turmoil to escape into the past & recall our happy care-free existences. I am a New Yorker, but have gravitated into this bull's eye, under the mistaken impression that it was too hidden to attract, ignoring the fact that my particular strip of coast, was the first land captured by the British in 1812![114]

The federal government restricted Hoffman's entire island estate, as it had installed a practice bombing range on several of the islands in Bogue Sound.

Hoffman, "in an effort to increase 'morale,'"[115] opened her home in World War II to soldiers stationed on Bogue Banks and at nearby Cherry Point Marine Air Station. The 101st Infantry patrolled the beaches on the island, and the 244th Artillery maintained guns along the first set of dunes near the beach. Hoffman's home was the scene for frequent parties given for the soldiers. Besides parties, Hoffman also welcomed overnight visitors and soldiers who presented themselves at mealtimes. Often, local fisherman caught the food and served it right out of the water, with the soldiers volunteering to help. Apparently, soldiers later recalled their stay on the island and wrote to her long after the war ended. Hoffman received this poem from one young Marine who had visited her Bogue Banks home:

At the edge of the forest, by the banke of the Sound
Alone & secluded, there may be found,
Aloof, yet inviting, enchanting Bogue Banks
Apart & protected from humanity's pranks.

The waves of her moat lap at her slim feet,
The trees of her battlements guard peace complete
Inspired & bewitching to but a favored few
Her stations are all manned by a faithful crew.

With the Princess to watch over all daily cares,
And a Princess she is, yet without any airs,
While around her still chambers, with her mind in the skies
Waits the Queen of Bogue Banks, though both worldly & wise.[116]

Hoffman, however, never became a part of the Carteret County community. At opposite extremes of American culture and society, neither Hoffman nor the coastal Carolinians wished to change their natures. Local residents often treated Hoffman with suspicion and distrust. In a letter to one of her New York attorneys, Hoffman explained that in dealing with her Carteret County lawyers on a matter of taxation, he would find both of them "very illusive . . . they do not wish to appear to champion a Northerner."[117] Hoffman was even rumored to be a German spy during the war who "radioed freighter positions to waiting German submarines off the North Carolina coast."[118] A companion of Hoffman's, Gabrielle Brard, recalled, "At one time, we were under suspicion. I heard that the Army was investigating Mrs. Hoffman and myself. She was an outsider and I was a foreigner [from Paris]. During a time of war, an investigation of us did not seem illogical. I remember finding evidence of soldiers who had been watching the house."[119] Brard prevailed upon Hoffman's attorney of the time, Frank M. Wooten, to request the Federal Bureau of Investigation to investigate the rumors to learn their source. Wooten wrote that "Hoffman [had] lived in France for about forty years, this with her name seems to be the principal cause of the rumors."[120] An agent of the FBI replied that, although Wooten's letter had been noted, it was impossible for the agency to make the suggested investigation.[121]

Hoffman's patriotism seemed beyond reproach, and she supported the war effort. Hoffman received Eugen Millington-Drake, British minister to Uruguay during the war and a lifelong friend, as a guest at Bogue Banks on his way to Great Britain to take part in a conference concerning the relations between North and South America. Hoffman wrote to an American radio station which broadcast programs to Europe, chiding them on their choice of music: "How can any self respecting patriotic American wish an international audience to suppose that such a program is either representative or pleasing to our compatriots . . . We have composers in America . . . If we try again, let's give them something to listen to. Who compares with Sousa?"[122] Nevertheless, due to her eccentricity and aloofness, unsubstantiated stories still circulated about Hoffman's traitorous spy activities.

Hoffman's greater problem in Carteret County concerned the people of the small fishing community who lived on her property. Residents of Salter Path trace their ancestors' ties to the isolated location back some time before the 1850s. Fishermen from the mainland built fish camps during the late summer and early fall to fish during the seasonal run of mullet along the beach. Soon, a few families of Willises and Guthries stayed on the island and established homes. "The community adopted the name Salter Path from a path which ran from the sound to the ocean belonging to a Mr. Salter."[123]

A court proceeding in 1854 at the county seat in Beaufort to determine a title on Bogue Banks indicated that people other than the parties involved in the case lived on the island. Court records noted that "the names indicate that these persons are the ancestors of the persons who now live in the Village of Salter Path. These persons were made parties defendant to this proceeding."[124] An indirect reference to them was made in 1880. In the fall of that year, "a young biologist named R. Edward Earll toured local fisheries in some of the remotest sections of the North Carolina coast. He had a special interest in the large mullet fishery based on the barrier islands of Carteret County."[125] A definite reference was made when in 1908, Collier Cobb, a University of North Carolina geologist, visited mullet camps in Carteret County, including one at Rice Path on Bogue Banks.[126] Fisherman used Rice Path, located at the western end of Salter Path, to haul mullet from the beach to the village. These first settlers built wood frame houses with only one or two rooms filled with homemade furniture. Robert Sullivan, a reporter from a New York newspaper, wrote, "Their houses are built in a crazy scattering around a knob on the backbone of the island. Since nobody owns a lot, the buildings apparently were put up the way the pile of lumber happened to fall. Some are back to back, some face to face, others turn their backs impolitely on neighbors."[127] They used kerosene or whale oil lamps for light. Pine straw filled their mattresses. The women in the small community made their clothes, quilts, and soap. The men hunted and fished. Families raised chickens, pigs, and vegetables. Most families owned a cow or cows which roamed freely on the banks. There were no roads until the 1940s; the inhabitants used paths to get from one house to another through the thick vegetation and boats to take the infrequent trips to the mainland.

Carteret County did not start recording births until 1913. After that year, however, many people had previous births recorded at the county seat. The earliest birth records in Salter Path date to the 1890s: John Wesley Frost was born November 28, 1891; Wallace A. Guthrie, August 14, 1897; Lena Willis, August 23, 1897.[128] Marriage records in the county were kept sparsely throughout the 1800s. The earliest records of marriage taking place in Salter Path also date to the 1890s: Edwin Willis and Wealthy E. Guthrie, married by R.C. Bell, JP, November 12, 1891; John H. Willis and Annie Guthrie, married by Cas. F. Stevens, minister, September 1, 1895; Josephus Lewis and Lula Willis, married by John S. Warren, minister, April 19, 1897.[129] It is reasonable to assume that if marriages and births took place in Salter Path in the 1890s, that the village had been established well before that date.

The small community remained fairly static until a great hurricane in 1899 hit the North Carolina coast and brought a resettlement of Outer Banks inhabitants. David Stick, author of *The Outer Banks of North Carolina*, stated that the destructive hurricane completely demolished the settlement of Diamond City, located on Shackleford Banks near Cape Lookout. Author Joel Hancock concurred, noting that "the wind and tides of the south Atlantic . . . rang a death knell for the several communities that had grown and flourished on what had been a comfortable and hospitable island."[130] The inhabitants, who lived almost exclusively by whaling and salvaging cargo off the beach from wrecked ships, moved to Promise Land in Morehead City or nearby Harkers Island. Stick noted, however, "Most of the folks on the other end of Shackleford Banks went down to Bogue Banks, to a place called Gillikin, now known as Salter Path, and their children live there still."[131]

The people of Salter Path lived simply and took care of one another. Any family in real need relied on the community for help. The men beach fished together, although divided into several crews, with older men as captains and younger men doing most of the hard work. They shared profits. Infrequently, the men had to force a lazy man to work. When this occurred, the man's wife and family received his share, so even the few ne'er-do-wells had enough to eat. A Raleigh, North Carolina newspaper article contained a description of the inhabitants:

> They call their village Salter Path . . . It is without any formal being. It has no mayor, no courts, no laws. It has never known the necessity for them for they have had other ways of maintaining themselves as a community. They have had a very practical form of socialism in which there was no theory. They have never had any theory about it, only necessity. There has never been any riot there, and no blood has been spilled because there were those who opposed the ideal of socialism and the brotherhood of man. They have been brothers because they had to be brothers or perish.[132]

The reporter added that the villagers recalled little concerning their past or their cooperative efforts. They spoke only of the necessity of working together to make a living from the sea.

When Hoffman bought her Bogue Banks property, Salter Path numbered about two hundred inhabitants. The community consisted of houses, fish and scallop houses, a Methodist church, a small store, and a school with grades one through seven. When the postal service first began to address mail there, collected in Morehead City and brought over by boat, for want of a name (as people were scattered all along the banks), it called Salter Path "Gillikin" after the village schoolteacher, Betty Gillikin.

This, then, was the village that Hoffman acquired with her land purchase. Royall, the former owner of the land that held the community, never interfered with the people in Salter Path, although he came into infrequent contact with some of the men out fishing or hunting. Hoffman, though, decided to enter into the life of the village.

At first, Hoffman gave gifts to the members of the community of clothes, shoes, and food. These hand-outs, not actually needed or appreciated, were offered at the price of restrictions placed upon them. The people were to cut no wood for fire, stop their cattle from freely grazing, and give Hoffman two shares of their fishing profits. Hoffman had a notice put in the local paper which read:

> NOTICE - Bogue Banks
>
> Any person and all persons owning or interested in any stock whether hogs, cattle, sheep or other stock-which is now running at large or which may heretofore have been permitted on the premises of John A. Royall, now the property of Mrs. Hoffman on Bogue Banks, are HEREBY NOTIFIED and required promptly to remove said stock from said premises. Premises mentioned is all that land extending from ocean to sound just east of Salter Path and down to the eastern line of said property at Yeopon [Yaupon] Point. A portion of said premises is now fenced and the remainder is being fenced; and any and all stock not removed prior the 1st day of June, 1918, will be proceeded against in accordance with the law. This 16th day of April, 1918. Mrs. Hoffman, Owner. By J.F. Duncan.[133]

Before two years had ended, Hoffman had aroused the anger and resentment of the Salter Path people. They refused to abide by the restraints on their freedom, continuing to live as they always had. Perhaps one peacemaker from the community, McCajah Adams wrote:

> Dear Mrs Hoffman, I have been informed that there has been quite alot of talk to you in regards to the people at this place. Some of it is true and some of the talk is not true. There has [*sic*] been some obligations made you by the people here and they did not keep their promise and some did. I will be to see you soon and if there is anything I can help you to I will be pleased to do so. With best wishes.[134]

Hoffman demanded Royall to take action against the settlers, as he had sold her the property. Royall, in hopes of placating Hoffman, placed a trespass notice in the paper, warning all from entering the property on Bogue Banks that had once belonged to him. Royall's response to Hoffman's demands made through her New York attorneys reveal her usual behavior. He wrote:

> Mrs. Hoffman commenced to cause me trouble from the moment she became a tenant of mine on the Island, and that fact is responsible, in a large measure, for the ultimate sale of the property to her in 1917. I did not seek to sell her this property; she begged me to let her have it, and afterwards, in the presence of Mr. Satterlee, before papers were drawn, insisted that I include Salter Path in her purchase, for the reason, as she stated, she had become very much attached to these simple people and intended to do more for them than I had ever done, and I believed her. She took over from me a peaceful situation, filled with good will toward her, but unfortunately, for all concerned, it did not last long.
>
> I sold her a highly valuable piece of property at a very low price, upon easy terms of payment, as she told me at the time it was the only way she could hope to own it. I am free to confess that if I were its owner to-day, three times what she paid me for it in 1917 would not buy it, and this without the improvements she has placed upon it.
>
> Unfortunately for Mrs. Hoffman, she is largely responsible for her own troubles, and I must say has her own peculiar ideas of justice. [135]

To further complicate the relationship between Hoffman and the villagers, David John Willis, representative for the entire population of Salter Path, filed a claim in court for ownership of her property from the community to McGinnis Point, approximately five miles eastward and close to her house. A Beaufort attorney, Claude Wheatly, represented Willis. Infuriated that the problem with the villagers had been allowed to progress to this point, Hoffman wrote her overseer:

> I have just received your wire about David John. They will be worse than ever until the matter is settled in the courts. I am sorry that Mr Royall & Mr Duncan have not proceeded before, it would have made the matter easier to settle, as they undoubtedly have fallen into the hands of some lawyer who needs money! The result of D.J.'s summons makes

> me think that the authorities in Beaufort are tired of having me down there![136]

Willis's suit was never properly decided in court and records for it are not available.[137]

Hoffman had a change of heart concerning the village and never offered them help again. Although some of the men had worked for her from time to time, she advised her property overseer to stop hiring them. She wrote:

> I do not want any S.P. men to work for me if you can do without them, I mean if you can get any better people. I think it poor policy to engage them unless it is very much to our advantage . . . I am so glad that you understand them now yourself, & can judge how best to handle them. Each one needs a different method, but the greatest mischief of the men is D.J. [David John Willis]. Do be on your guard with him.[138]

Hoffman decided to take serious measures against the Salter Path people. She wrote Julius Duncan, one of her Beaufort attorneys, asking him to accompany Royall and her to the village to post notices which read:

> Mrs. Hoffman shall receive for the fishing two shares.
>
> No green wood shall be cut or burned in the Community.
>
> No one shall trespass on her property from the line to the East of Salter Path to her eastern boundary.
>
> No cattle, hogs, horses, sheep, goats or any other livestock shall be allowed within these lines.
>
> No one shall interfere in any way with her property or the people in her employ.
>
> In case any of the members of the Community are unwilling to be guided by the above requests it is understood that they will leave the village of Salter Path before the 1st of September, 1919.

> If at any time it should be found that any one had broken his agreement he would expect to be dispossessed without further notice. June 1919[139]

Duncan did not show, but Hoffman hoped that "Royall was at last convinced of the very unbecoming manner in which [she] was received there, & the defiance expressed by the spokesman of the village."[140] In the same letter, Hoffman related to Duncan that a man named Julian Brown had come to buy a cow from her, but she refused to sell him one unless he also took a small red cow which she had confiscated from a Salter Path resident. Brown agreed on bartering goats for the red cow. Brown, however, promptly informed a Salter Path man of Hoffman's intention to sell the cow, and he, with others, came and took the cow from her place. Hoffman declared that she was still holding Brown responsible for his end of the bargain and asked Duncan to "write him that to avoid trouble he must bring the barter without delay. I cannot permit these S.P. [Salter Pathers] to laugh at me."[141] Due to her thoughtless, heavy-handed dealings with the villagers, who had been free on the banks for decades, Hoffman's problems with Salter Path were just beginning.

Chapter Three

Fishing and Farming

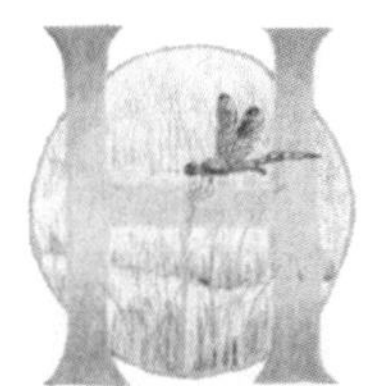

offman bought her North Carolina home for relaxation and pride, but she wanted her island estate to be self-sufficient and also hoped to make a profit from it. This was soon after another New Yorker, Henry Flagler, built a railroad from the North to Miami and Key West and erected luxurious resort hotels in St. Augustine, Palm Beach, Miami, and other Florida cities. What did Bogue Banks have to offer Hoffman? Although she cleared only the underbrush from the immediate area of Shore House, leaving the large trees, apparently she had no reservations on the cutting of trees on other portions of her property. Immediately after purchasing her land, she brought in a timber expert, Max Jaspon, to measure it for timber. Although her employees frequently dynamited trees to clear parts of the property, Hoffman never managed to sell the timber rights, perhaps occupied with other ventures. As late as 1933, she still "looked forward to selling the sedar [*sic*], or starting some industry which would be helpful."[142]

Another scheme Hoffman considered was drilling for oil. In 1930, after a discussion with E.H. Gorham, one of her Beaufort attorneys, she sent data concerning her property to a Mr. Norris and asked for an opinion on the probability of finding oil. She told him she had found "a peculiar opalescent oily spume [which] was the result of watering some very parched ground just opposite [her] house."[143] She also related a story of a fish kill at Bogue Inlet on the west end of Bogue Banks after the appearance of what seemed to be oil on the water's surface. Hoffman noted, "I have always understood from those who think they know that it is said that this property resembles in appearance the Texas Oil wells."[144] Mr. Norris apparently did not reply, and there is no further mention of oil on Hoffman's land.

Likewise, Hoffman hoped to benefit from the numerous shipwrecks which occurred in the shallow ocean waters off Bogue Banks. Along the coastline of North Carolina—known as the Graveyard of the Atlantic—Diamond Shoals, Lookout Shoals, and Frying Pan Shoals stretch far into the ocean off the three capes (Hatteras, Lookout, and Fear), causing many maritime disasters. David Stick, in *Graveyard of the Atlantic*, mentions more than six hundred vessels that were lost off the coast and many others that were damaged. Along with flotsam, passing ships also left jetsam which was carried by waves to the beach. The inhabitants of the banks' villages made money from salvaging cargo, either selling it themselves or turning it over (for a reward) to agents of the insurance companies that insured the ships and owned the retrieved cargo.[145]

The people in Salter Path walked the beaches daily, looking for anything that had washed ashore. After her purchase of the island property, Hoffman attempted to change a long-standing practice by claiming all salvaged material for herself. She complained that the villagers "salvaged everything from the beach worth hundreds of dollars."[146] Often, she called for the county sheriff to force the villagers to hand over items found on the beach, which they would not willingly do. From Chicago, she wrote her Beaufort attorney, "My gardener writes me that a great deal of cylinder oil is coming ashore at Salter Park [*sic*]. He has bought two barrels for my personal use. I wish you would ask him how many barrels have been salvaged by the village. This property, of course, is by rights mine and that is one of the things that I want you to make clear to the people of Salter Park [*sic*]. I am not willing that they should appropriate anything that comes up on the beach."[147] Hoffman had very definite ideas about what belonged to her and to no one else.

The Salter Path men fished the sound waters for scallops, crabs, oysters, and clams, but the biggest cash crop for them was the annual run of mullet along the beach in late summer and throughout the fall. Writing from Beaufort in 1871, H.C. Yarrow noted:

> [mullet] is the most abundant of [fish] in the locality, and affords sustenance and employment to thousands of persons on the coast of North Carolina. . . . The numbers taken are simply enormous . . . It was estimated by competent observers that not less than 12,000 barrels of mullet were captured on the coast of North Carolina. Friday, September 22, 1871.[148]

This was the season the Salter Path men stayed on the beach in fish camps, with several of their wives cooking meals there for them. They made up four fishing crews: the "Redbird" crew, the Salter Path crew, the Belco [Bell's Cove] crew, and the "Tea

House" crew. The "Tea House" camp was located across the island from Hoffman's Tea House on the sound. Derisively, the fishermen would say they were "going down to the Tea House," until the name caught on and remained.

Hoffman wanted the profits from the mullet catches and attempted to drive the Salter Path fishing crews from the beach if they did not comply. She planned to sell the fishing rights to another company.[149] "In 1920 the Ocean Leather Company formed by northern interests built a [processing] plant some three miles west of Morehead City along Bogue Sound where sharks were skinned and the livers refined."[150] As the villagers ignored her claims and continued to fish, Hoffman relented on her initial demand of the complete rights to fish the beach and instead, claimed two shares of every catch as owner of the property.[151] The fishermen, however, refused to pay her any part at all. Hoffman wrote one of her Beaufort attorneys from Chicago, requesting him to make certain that she receive her shares. Her lawyer, Julius Duncan replied, "You surely are aware of the fact that I can not be personally cognizant of the happenings there [Salter Path]," but Hoffman answered:

> Of course, it is impossible for me, at this distance, to tell you what is taking place at Salter Park [*sic*], but we agreed that the signature of every one in the village should be required, and had you obtained the signatures you could not fail to have learned that the fishing has been going on ever since I called it to your attention at the end of April.[152]

The sheriff of Carteret County informed Duncan that the Salter Path men had held a meeting about Hoffman's demand that they either share fishing or leave the island; they refused to do either. Hoffman then ordered Duncan to have the Salter Path fishermen arrested for trespassing, but strangely, the deputy sheriffs could never find anyone from the village fishing on the beach. Hoffman attempted to enlist the help of her overseer, Sam Duplanty, in forcing the villagers to abide by her stipulation. She promised Duplanty, "I will give you half of what I receive from the fishing, that is to say, one of the shares I require them to pay for fishing from the village."[153] According to his daughter, Claire Manfredi, Duplanty refused. Manfredi noted, "My father never bothered them (Salter Path folks) and needless to say we had plenty of seafood."[154] Hoffman, however, wrote, "The S.P.s are catching the most enormous lot of fish and Sam has been explaining how we can make money at it without having any of the bother. . . . As soon as I have an artesian well and an ice-plant it will not be necessary to go to M.C. (Morehead City) at all. We can even ship our fish from our own station . . . I begin to believe that it can be made a source of wealth."[155]

Hoffman attempted to make a deal with Harvey Willis of Salter Path. The two entered into a contract which gave Willis the "privilege of fishing along the ocean from of her property from Salter Path on Bogue Banks one mile east at what is called or known as Plank Path."[156] In return, Willis "will pay as rent to the said Mrs. Hoffman Four (4) shares weekly from the proceeds of the sale of fish caught, the shares to be calculated in the usual manner as done in Carteret County . . . in the event the said Mrs. Hoffman agrees to buy the fishing equipment to carry on the said work of fishing then she is to receive as rent for the same ten (10) shares."[157] Duplanty informed Hoffman, however, that "Harvey cannot get a crew to fish at S.P. as Geo. Smith and H. Willis has [*sic*] been telling around that you was [*sic*] only doing it for spite and trying to starve them out."[158]

Hoffman "gave up all idea of attempting to come to any kind of terms with the Salter Path people and decided instead to go in partnership with Mr. [Llewellyn] Phillips, who has one of odorous [*sic*] fertilizer factories and needed only fish to transform into a product which is sold for cash and has jumped from $23 to $40 a ton in the last month."[159]

On August 1, 1932 Phillips had obtained the Newport Fisheries Company's fish factory, plant, and equipment at bankruptcy proceedings. Phillips paid $2,701 for the operation, located on Starvation Island in the Newport River between Morehead City and Beaufort.[160]

Hoffman put up notices prohibiting the villagers from fishing on the beach at all. She then arranged to supply fishing gear to a crew of other Carteret County fishermen and have them fish for a weekly wage. Later, however, Hoffman wrote that the Salter Path men "told my partner in the fishing contract last year that if he attempted to fish on my beach for me he would 'wade through blood,' with the result that he broke his contract costing me thousands of dollars."[161]

It was clear that Hoffman would receive only with great difficulty aid from anyone in Carteret County. She attempted to involve her New York City lawyers in the fight, stating:

> There can be no question whatever that fishing rights which are acknowledged by all the wholesale dealers in the City (who go as far as Texas to collect their fish) to be the finest on the Atlantic Coast should be at the disposal of the owner and the fact that I have been prevented from exercising those rights through the menaces of the inhabitants living on my property by my bounty ought to be vindicated by some legal precedent.[162]

Hoffman's New York lawyers could do nothing to help her with her problems in North Carolina except recommend a local attorney: Hoffman had already engaged two Beaufort attorneys. Although she owned twelve miles of beach property with a wide flat beach that was perfect for fishing, bought expensive fishing gear, and had a partner with a fish factory to process fertilizer, which was much in demand in the agricultural South, Hoffman could find no one willing to fish for her.

By far, Hoffman's largest and costliest business project on Bogue Banks was the farm she established there in 1917, which she named Pine Grove Farms. She later wrote that she began the dairy farm for "patriotic reasons . . . with the desire & expectation of sending some really fine animals to replace the devastations committed by the germans [*sic*] early in the war."[163] She wanted to ship pedigreed cattle to France and apparently investigated the market in Carteret County as well, as she hoped to sell her dairy products locally. Hoffman also gave another explanation for the farm's establishment, the passage of the Sixteenth Amendment to the Constitution in 1913, which gave Congress the right to tax income. Throughout the years, Pine Grove Farms operated at a loss, which her accountant, stated Hoffman, "Arranged to come off my future income tax, which of course is one of the reasons that I go on farming for I would rather spend my money that way than paying taxes."[164]

Carteret County in 1920, woefully behind the rest of the state in farm production, ranked 98th among the state's one hundred counties in the number of dairy cattle on farms. H.C. Lay, agricultural expert within North Carolina's university system, noted that due to a lack of milk in their diet, "many [school] children in the county were found undernourished and underweight-some children as much as forty pounds underweight."[165] Hoffman hoped to benefit from the shortages of milk and butter. When the farm first got under way, she noted that "there is a tremendous demand for all my dairy products & I can sell without any middle man, which is the eldorado [*sic*] of trade. The public take skimmed milk, butter made from cream thereof & pay ten cents for buttermilk in the last resort. It is very encouraging."[166]

Although Hoffman took an active role in the establishment of Pine Grove Farms, she needed a permanent agricultural expert as farm manager, as she was often away from North Carolina. Two years after her purchase of the Bogue Banks property, Hoffman petitioned the Department of Agriculture's representative in Raleigh, North Carolina, for help in locating a competent farmer and businessman to manage the entire farm. She offered a "large bungalo [*sic*] without modern conveniences [as] a home" and added that she was "willing to pay the market value, with milk & farm privileges."[167] The Department of Agriculture had no one to recommend, but sent William Moore, North Carolina State Veterinarian, to inspect Hoffman's herd. After a thorough examination of her animals, Moore wrote her, "You have indeed secured some fine animals. . . . You should in a very short time build up a wonderful herd."[168]

Hoffman soon received a letter from the North Carolina College of Agriculture asking if she wanted to put her herd in its care. She consented and the college supervised the herd for several months. She, however, complained that the college's agents unnecessarily destroyed several of her animals while testing for tuberculosis. After she received a letter stating that their treasury did not have funds to pay the one hundred dollars guaranteed for each destroyed animal, Hoffman became dissatisfied and decided to assist at the next post mortem. Later, she recalled: "It was a very warm morning, but I stood beside the operator through all the harrowing hours of seeing him kill one of the loveliest little bulls I had ever bred."[169] Hoffman claimed that the operator found no tuberculosis and that she never heard from the college again.[170]

In 1919, Hoffman hired Sam Duplanty, a New Yorker, as farm manager. His daughter remembered:

> My mother became very ill and doctors told my father to move to a warm climate. He had a business with his nephew called 'Package Dispatch', similar to today's UPS. I don't know who told my father about a Mrs. Alice Hoffman, but here is where Bogue Banks enters our lives.
>
> Mrs. Hoffman owned Bogue Banks from Glover's Place through Salter Path. She did not know what to do with it, so she was looking for

> someone who could help her. . . . My father went to Bogue Banks to see her. I don't know what transpired, but sometime later he sent for my mother and me. . . . There were a lot of things that seemed strange to us, but now that I think of it, we were strange to everyone until they became used to us. We were 'Yankees'.[171]

Duplanty had no practical experience as manager of a dairy farm. Before his mail delivery business, he had owned and managed a hotel in San Francisco. However, a short relationship between Hoffman and Duplanty, as owner and superintendent of Pine Grove Farms, began. Duplanty's wife, Maggie, became housekeeper for the estate.

Duplanty tended to the farm operations while Hoffman attended various cattle auctions all over the country. She consulted sale catalogs distributed before each auction, hoping to obtain the best animals at bargain prices. At one auction "She agreed with the catalogue, that a young bull about six months old was as fine a specimen as had ever been offered at auction."[172] Hoffman secured the animal for $5,000, writing Duplanty that he would be "wild with delight when [he] sees the new arrivals."[173]

Hoffman and Duplanty hired local men as day laborers who dynamited and cleared trees and enclosed the areas for pasture. They erected several barns and dairy buildings, purchased a tractor, and in general, set about "making the farm a showplace."[174]

Hoffman also had plans for her mainland property. She wrote, "I want to establish a dairy, as there is none here, on the Mainland [*sic*] across from my place which would bring all kinds of advantages in its wake. . . . If I don't get control of the shore opposite & it is sold for small bungalos [*sic*], it will absolutely ruin my place as far as intrinsic value is concerned."[175] Hoffman and Duplanty began dairy operations on her mainland property, located in Mansfield. In 1926, a fire insurance policy on Hoffman's buildings listed coverage for, on the island, the main dwelling, farmer's residence, gardener's cottage, forester's cottage, teahouse, pine court, easterly shore cottage, pump house, wood shed, store house, dairy barn, barn H, barn J and, on the mainland, the dairy house, milk house, farmer's cottage, westerly shore cottage, garage, and mule house. Altogether, these structures were insured for $42,700.[176]

Brown, Crosby & Company, Inc. of New York City issued this insurance policy to Hoffman and added that it would "be helpful to see Mr. Gillikin and find out definitely if there is any insurance on the Fords."[177] Gillikin was Hoffman's automobile insurance agent in Morehead City. Hoffman still often neglected to pay her bills, as evident in the letter she received from Gillikin: "On Sept. 22nd 1924 I issued policy on your auto premium[$] 27.35. I do not think you have treated me right, it does not bother you to remit for your accts but-it is hard for me to carry them as I am a poor man."[178]

Before hiring Duplanty, Hoffman lost cattle not only to the Agricultural College's slaughter of her animals, but also to her own neglect and carelessness. Dissatisfied with her initial selections of poor stock, good only for manure, Hoffman determined to begin the herd again with only the best cattle; she decided to purchase the breed of Holstein-Friesian, large black and white cows that produce more milk than any other breed of dairy cow. Hoffman purchased a prize bull named Dutchland Pietertje Cleary for $2,000 as sire for a quality herd from the F.F. Field Holstein Company, in Brockton, Massachusetts, "Home of the World's Greatest Producing Dams." Hoffman, who insisted upon building a herd with uniform color markings, wrote the president of the company that she regretted the dark color of a bull he had sold her. On all her cattle, she wanted a conventional black stripe in the middle with white legs and shoulders. Hoffman assured him, however, that she would use him "in the hope that he may throw back to his maternal great grand sire," whom she greatly admired.[179] Hoffman's prize bull, as well as another pedigreed bull, King Mata Jan Segis Aaggie, performed well at Pine Grove Farms, siring cattle which were given names such as Clara Segis Pontiac Prilly, Alcartra Segis Walker Prilly, Vance Cornicopia Segis, Jane de Kol Ormsby Abbekirk, King Mata Rag Apple Vale Pudmina, King Inka Vale Artis de Kol. Hoffman, disappointingly, could not induce local farmers to pay for her bull's services, owing, as she noted, to the inaccessibility of the island.

Hoffman also hired a New Yorker, William Woodward, to travel to Buffalo, New York, for a week or two and learn about the mixing of special feeds for cattle there and then to come to Bogue Banks to assist Duplanty with the herd. Woodward was to take charge especially of the butter-making, which would leave Maggie, who had been supervising the operation, freer to care for the household needs.

Hoffman closely supervised affairs at Pine Grove Farms when she was there and when absent, carried on continuous correspondence with Duplanty, providing him with books and pamphlets on farming. She encouraged him to keep the farm grounds and dairy buildings clean, wash the cows off after every milking with warm water, and increase the cattle's feed mixture to their highest consumption capacity. Hoffman wrote Duplanty while traveling by train to New York that she thought they should get sixty pounds of butter a week from their best three cows alone. She added, "Well, Sam, I think you have done splendidly, every letter tells of something new accomplished."[180]

Hoffman and Duplanty also raised pigs, chickens, and turkeys, and purchased lambs and goat kids. Duplanty made wine from the local muscadine grapes which grew in profusion on the banks. Hoffman also increased the population of her livestock by confiscating those animals which belonged to the Salter Path villagers but roamed unto her property. Hoffman wrote, "We are buying pigs from the S.P. people each time that they break in. The last he [Sam] got from Henry Willis. Two big ones for which he asked $40, Sam gave him $16."[181] They also planted large vegetable and fruit gardens.

Hoffman discovered that, as the Department of Agriculture included North Carolina in an agriculturally restricted area, none of her cattle could be certified for shipment to France until they had been dipped for ticks. Duplanty and the farm hands fashioned a large tank for the procedure. Interested in every aspect of the farm, Hoffman was on hand to watch and wrote, "Finally my Great King Mata came towards the tank & I pressed closer to lose nothing of the coming sight. As he dropped in, the water rose in a solid sheet & drenched me from head to feet. I retired in some confusion."[182]

Extremely proud of her farming operations, Hoffman wrote to an agricultural expert in Connecticut, James Connell, asking him for some advice concerning the farm and also offering him the position of superintendent. She described the dairy farm in detail and wanted him to make a visit to Bogue Banks to see it firsthand and give recommendations. Connell had serious doubts even before leaving for North Carolina:

> How did you happen to make such a large investment, in land, in that state? How did you happen to choose dairy cattle-Holsteins and why did you purchase such high-priced specimens, and why from the Oliver Cabana Jr. herd, whose reputation was not of the best. Why did you build a model dairy plant, place those valuable cattle on a comparatively undeveloped farm, in a tick area, and then placed the whole business in charge of a man, who, from what you say, knows little about agriculture?[183]

Hoffman was to hear more pointed and disgusted opinions from James Connell after his visit to Bogue Banks.

For a while, Hoffman's farm showed some evidence of success. The farm workers carried milk to the market in Morehead City in Hoffman's car along her private road. Hoffman continued to attend cattle auctions, purchasing Holstein-Friesian in order to build up a creditable pedigreed herd. She and Duplanty looked to expand the dairy operations on the island and the mainland. As well as the cattle she shipped to France, Hoffman sold some cows to the North Carolina School for the Deaf and Blind in Raleigh. But trouble soon surrounded her from all sides.

The Salter Path villagers continued to cause Hoffman problems on her farm. They still hunted on her property as they always had. Hoffman maintained, "It is their precept & practice that in all things they shall do as they did before I bought my property. . . . They take especial attention in shooting near enough to the house to attract attention."[184] She added that "the very fact of their suggesting that I should divide my place in half & allow them to enjoy the use of half of such an estate shows that they are not logical & cannot be treated like responsible persons."[185]

Hoffman requested John Royall to abide by his promise to give her the first option to buy the remainder of the western end of the island. She wanted to move the villagers there and erect "some kind of barrier which it will be impossible for the people to climb or deface without committing a misdemeanor punishable by imprisonment."[186] Royall, having his fill of Hoffman, sold the property to Henry K. Fort, an importer/exporter from Philadelphia. This sale brought Hoffman more problems in the future.

Soon after Hoffman's request to Royall, she brought charges of trespassing against two Salter Path men, Henry Willis and David John Willis. She, in turn, was summoned to appear in the county court in Beaufort in answer to a charge of theft made by David John Willis. Willis demanded restitution for a hog caught on Hoffman's property and impounded by Duplanty. The court in Beaufort dismissed the charge of trespassing for want of jurisdiction, stating that the defendants were tenants at will of the plaintiff. Willis's charge of theft was also dismissed, but Hoffman had to pay court costs.[187] Hoffman complained again to Royall:

> It is very surprising that I should lose a case in Beaufort for trying to protect myself against the losses caused by the stock of Salter Path. . . . It would seem as if the Beaufort legal lights preferred marauders to law abiding citizens.[188]

Hoffman blamed Royall for taking the position that the villagers were harmless, berating him for the loss of pleasure that she had anticipated from her sojourns on the island. Stymied, as she could not have the entire village arrested, Hoffman anxiously noted that "if it should ever occur to them that a stray shot in a window would go unpunished I am not prepared to say that they would be above firing it."[189]

Hoffman suspected the villagers also for the loss of many of her chickens. She wrote to her secretary, "My hens are dying of a mysterious malady which Munroe [a farm worker] thinks is poison!!! I now care only for fish freshly caught, & do not even feel like eggs which you will understand. . . . Maggie thinks the hens are poisoned & suggests that the stock may be next to go."[190]

James Connell, meanwhile, arrived in North Carolina to consider the job of farm manager that Hoffman had offered him. As indicated by his assessment of Hoffman's problems with the Salter Path inhabitants, Connell must have remained on Bogue Banks for a considerable amount of time. Hoffman was not prepared for Connell's letter of refusal, written upon his return to his home in Connecticut:

> There is an element in my makeup which prevents my doing, or participating in that which I do not believe to be right, proper, or for the best. . . . My stay at Bogue Banks and rambles about the mainland were to see the Salterpath [*sic*] settlement, and Bogue Island [*sic*] itself.[191]

Connell informed Hoffman that her island estate appeared more a playground and residence than a dairy farm. He thought perhaps it might be appropriate for a golf course. Connell then castigated Hoffman for his real interest in her farm operations:

> Twenty cents per quart is too high a price for standard milk. Milk is sold by the farmers about here [Connecticut] for not more than eight cents and often less. Is any milk used by the Salterpath [*sic*] children. and

> if so, where obtained? Somehow I feel that you are morally bound to help those people, and I am not altogether in sympathy with your attempt to dispossess them of their homes. Does their presence materially injure you?
>
> I cannot banish from my mind the thought that you can do much for those Salterpath people, your neighbors on the mainland, and even for the poor children in Morehead City, whose parents cannot afford to pay 20 cents for milk. These, and not the dollars and cents questions, might be sufficient inducements for me to further consider the matter of going down there.[192]

In elitist tones, Hoffman promptly responded:

> There is something in my 'makeup' which claims to correct wrong impressions. . . . I am doing all that I can to prevent the development of Bogue Island into another Coney Island. I feel that there are places enough for the masses, without sacrificing the most beautiful beach in that vicinity. . . . I do not think the usual atmosphere of Motion Pictures, Dance Halls, Golf Courses & in general the accessories which the crowd find indispensable in order to be amused are desirable. . . .
>
> In connection with the village of Salter Path . . . several members went on the witness stand & claimed the entire property thus 'clouding' my title. . . . their cattle have been allowed to roam so continually on my place that I am compelled to dip my cattle. . . . When the Court sent the Surveyor to put up permanent markers showing the boundaries, they were destroyed the same day, although I was obliged to pay for the work. . . . They openly defy the Court. . . . This will explain why I am not interested in supplying the children with milk at a loss.[193]

Although Connell asked Hoffman to keep him apprised of the situation on Bogue Banks, needless to say, Hoffman never corresponded with him again.

As early as 1920, disease appeared in Hoffman's dairy herd. While she visited in New York, Duplanty informed her that a cow named Winooski had died after a sickness. Hoffman instructed Duplanty to clean out the dead cow's stall and thoroughly disinfect it because otherwise their milk sales would be ruined. Nevertheless, Hoffman bought another bull and planned more and larger buildings.

In the yearly testing for tuberculosis, a state inspector found the disease in one of Hoffman's cows. According to Hoffman, the cow scheduled to be slaughtered died and had to be buried before the Department of Agriculture's local inspector showed up to conduct the post-mortem. After the inspector's unsatisfactory visit, Hoffman wrote Dr. Brookbank, head of the Department of Agriculture's North Carolina office in Raleigh that he never send Dr. Dendinger to her place again. Hoffman complained that she had had to board the doctor and his wife at her expense, although he stayed in a hotel. She also claimed that Dr. Dendinger told the wife of the hotel proprietor that he had found tuberculosis in her herd. Hoffman wrote that "these people are so ignorant that they do not know it is a safeguard to get their milk from a herd which is under state supervision and since Dr. Dendinger's remark I have sold no milk in Morehead City. This behavior is outrageous."[194]

Nearly all Hoffman's cattle had to be destroyed because of the infectious disease. Although the animals were insured with the Hartford Insurance Company against tuberculosis, Hoffman could not recover any money for them, because of a clause in the policy under "Exception, Section Four, the loss of cattle by TB when they are ordered destroyed by the authorities."[195] When Hoffman threatened legal action against the company, its representative wrote to her that she was wasting her time and money.

The highly infectious disease could have spread to Hoffman's employees who worked with the cattle or to persons who drank the milk. Hoffman, however, expressed her sadness at the loss of her herd:

> We have almost no cows left, Peibe was found dead in the woods. You will be sorry to hear, I am sure, that I have lost my beautiful Rag Apple Amy, my most beautiful possession. When I felt out of sorts I used to think of her & rejoice in her beauty. I am afraid I will never find anything I like so well. It is a great disappointment.[196]

Hoffman had the entire island farm cleaned, disinfected, inspected, and then set about replenishing the herd. Within a few months, Hoffman had bought several head of cattle and was prepared to begin dairy operations again. The farm on the mainland was not affected by the tuberculosis problem and continued to supply milk.

In 1921, however, new troubles began as Hoffman started having problems with the Duplantys. She complained, "Sam takes no interest in trying to improve in any branch of farming he does not understand, the cows are losing ground every day."[197] That there was some faulty communication between them is plain, for after Hoffman's remark, Duplanty informed her that all the cows were doing well and all were with calf except one named Maudie. Duplanty seemed to think that the farm was recovering nicely from its misfortunes.

From the early establishment of Pine Grove Farms until some time in 1923, the long string of correspondence between Hoffman and the Duplantys exhibited a strong rapport. They appeared to be in complete harmony concerning the problems with Salter Path. There was unlimited speculation about the work needed to make the farm profitable and a source of pride. Hoffman, often away from Bogue Banks, appeared to rely entirely on the Duplantys for the management of the household and farm, although she constantly issued orders and made suggestions. As owner, the right to do so belonged to her and the Duplantys evidently harbored no resentment for it.

In 1923, a mutual tone of resentment crept into their letters. Correspondence became reserved, rather than friendly and cooperative. For example, Hoffman and Duplanty had decided to build their own dock onshore for *Fred*, the motorboat. Hoffman complained that Duplanty, with characteristic unthoughtfulness, had made his wife's life simpler by building the dock in front of their cottage, whereas she had to trudge the distance from Shore House to reach it.

The cause for the disaffection, as with most of Hoffman's problems, rested on money. Hoffman had promised Duplanty a bonus, but never gave it. She wrote, "I realize that you have put in extra time, Sam, but the bonus that I promised to pay you should be some reward for that."[198] Duplanty wanted the money, not the promise.

Hoffman also owed Maggie Duplanty sixty dollars for butter money for four months and asked Duplanty to please deduct the butter money from his monthly allowance for the running of the farm and give it to his wife. Maggie answered:

> Your letter to Sam has caused no little discontent with him as he says he is absolutely discouraged in taking off the $60 from the allowance when he has not taken his salary for five months. He says there is no use to try to continue in this way & pay the bills on this small allowance & then take 60 from his wages which he had not had Sam says that . . . you promised to send him his bonos [*sic*] money when you returned to N.Y.[199]

In the attempt to straighten out the relationship, Maggie implored Hoffman not to let Duplanty know that she wrote because he had said he would never write again. Maggie added, "I feel very discouraged & disheartened [that] everything seems to be getting worse."[200]

Their correspondence, although more sparse, showed an improvement in their relationship for a time (perhaps Hoffman paid Duplanty his bonus and Maggie her butter money, although there is no record of it), but on February 17, 1926 Duplanty quit signing his letters to Hoffman "Sam" and began signing "SE Duplanty." On February 26, 1926, Sam informed Hoffman that he was leaving.

Again, Hoffman and the Duplantys appeared to have cleared up the problems between them, with Sam and Maggie staying on Bogue Banks for over another year. In May 1927, Hoffman wrote Miss Curtis, "After a more than usually violent altercation Maggie and Sam, that is to say Maggie . . . decided to part. . . . I am told by different people of this region that Sam made fabulous sums of money but Mr. Gorham says that he has been foreclosed in many instances and is very hard pushed just now."[201]

Hoffman lost, in Duplanty, perhaps her most able and patient farm supervisor. Duplanty and his wife, Maggie, befriended Hoffman, as well as performed their duties. Duplanty appeared genuine in his endeavor to make the dairy farm a "showplace." Problems stemmed from Hoffman's desire to own a superior establishment without spending the money needed for such an endeavor. Hoffman's relationships with her subsequent managers never reached the early congeniality of those with Duplanty.

Upon Duplanty's resignation, Hoffman hired a man named Monroe Lewis and his three sons from Marshallberg, North Carolina, to oversee her Bogue Banks dairy farm.[202] Lewis had worked for Hoffman under the management of Duplanty and attempted to operate the dairy efficiently, but Hoffman questioned his use of the allowance money she sent. Lewis wrote:

> I cannot understand why you have deducted . . . $25. . . . I have used every penny of last month's allowance in the statement I am sending you . . . I haven't even enough to pay the men. . . . In your letter you state that in future I shall have $45 a month for expenses. This, as you know Mrs. Hoffman, is quite impossible. . . . If the allowance is reduced to $45 I have no alternative but to send all the animals over to the Farm [the mainland farm?] as I will, under no circumstances, run the risk of being brought up by the S.P.C.A. who are already sufficiently on the alert. I have never kept any animal short of food and I cannot start now.[203]

Hoffman wanted Lewis, as Duplanty, to run the farm on a shoestring budget. By 1929, Hoffman thought that Lewis was working out well. She wrote Francis Curtis, "I have just come back from North Carolina where things seem to be going *very* satisfactorily with Munroe [*sic*] in charge."[204] Curiously, Hoffman noted that Monroe seemed interested in the farming, except that he had unnecessarily lost a number of animals that year owing to underestimating the feed supply. Hoffman hoped soon, however, to receive a certificate for Grade-A milk from the government inspector.

But, Hoffman had not heard the last from the Duplantys. Hoffman received a letter from John Judge, her New York attorney, which cautioned, "I strongly advise you to have nothing to do with Sam and his efforts to sue your property . . . You are rid of Sam, and stay so. Do not write him."[205] Although no suits are recorded in the Beaufort courthouse against Hoffman by Sam Duplanty, that is not the case with Maggie Duplanty.

On July 4,1927, Maggie Duplanty sent a letter to E.H. Gorham, Hoffman's attorney, stating, "Your letter received last night with check inclosed [*sic*] written 'Wages in full' to June 30 1927 which is not correct as I have the amount of $79.00 due me yet from 1925 & should I cash this check I would close my claim for that amount. This has been played upon others but will not go with me."[206] Duplanty wrote that she had "done work enough for three women" since Hoffman had been in North Carolina and informed Gorham that Hoffman's "last letter was so insulting to me that I have not been in the frame of mind to answer & dont [*sic*] expect to any time soon. Her injustice & ingratitude for all my efforts to have everything as she asked . . . is plain. . . . All I ask now is the balance of what is owing me."[207]

Hoffman, as in the past with other retainers, refused to pay Maggie Duplanty her wages. Finally, Duplanty filed suit against Hoffman who threatened:

> I shall go on the stand & say that she was in town for over a month on full wages . . . nor did a stroke of work after the 9th of May. . . . she had overridden herself, & I shall certainly do everything in my power to see that she gets what is coming to her. They have been a constant drain ever since I allowed them to take charge of the place.[208]

The records show that no one took the stand; the matter was settled out of court.[209]

Lewis left Pine Grove Farms sometime in 1928 and Hoffman hired a man from New York, E. Abbott, to manage the dairy for three hundred dollars a month. Hoffman noted that the farm had finally received certification to sell Grade-A milk, thus enabling top price for its products.

Hoffman, characteristically, began to have trouble with Abbott. After the loss of six cows and two mules within a year's time, she accused Abbott of allowing the animals to starve to death. She claimed to have a letter from the president of the Holstein-Frisian [*sic*] Association of Brattleboro, New York[210] which stated that Abbott had a record of unsavory character throughout that state, noting that she had employed him before looking into his past record and that she thought he was "collecting money for a get-away."[211]

Again, there is a discrepancy between Hoffman's letters and the letters of those same persons to her. Three months after Hoffman accused Abbott of stealing her farm allowance money, he wrote a letter to her concerning the farm while she visited her niece, Eleanor, in Puerto Rico. Abbott noted:

> What breaks a man's heart is to have a cow making high production, as I was doing in the fall, and then have to go without feed and as a consequence have her drop down. . . . As you know, about half the time I have not known for sure whether I was going to get any more feed. . . . I did keep a daily milk sheet but when I saw there was no use with the feed situation as it was, I quit.[212]

Hoffman spent almost the entire decade of the 1930s in France, returning to America only because she had lost her home in Paris and feared the rise of Nazi Germany in Europe. For some reason not found in her correspondence, Hoffman brought suit against E. Abbott in 1936. Of course, she failed to appear in court and the action was dismissed, with the plaintiff to pay court costs.[213]

Hoffman returned to Pine Grove Farms in April, 1938. Her final words on twenty years of this undertaking follow:

> The Farm has gone out of existence, having been foreclosed by the N.C. Joint Stock Land Bank, & not worth being enough to pay the taxes, much less the few thousands of dollars I had been industriously paying principal & interest for the past ten or fifteen years.
>
> The modern barn & equipment has been leaking for years, in the effort to become worthless! The engine room which was especially built to sterilize the bottles has fallen into disuse, because not only did the people not pay their milk bills, but they kept the bottles as well!!!
>
> After the foreclosure the representative of the J.S.L. Bank offered to give the farm away to whoever would accept it, but there were no takers.
>
> The only satisfaction I ever had from the whole enterprise was being able to send 15 head of registered cattle to the Liberated Regions after they were grown enough to make the journey.[214]

Pine Grove Farms ceased to exist, but Hoffman's North Carolina problems did not.

What was her purpose all those many years of farming? Was it only to send cattle to France and provide milk for people in Carteret County? That is what she first said, but perhaps all those years of working, scheming, and disputing with all around her were for another purpose. As an intelligent woman, she looked perhaps for verification that she could manage anything without help. Did she look for power and authority, a scepter, a crown? Already, it is difficult work to know who deceived whom in her relationships, but, as we will see, matters become even more confusing.

Chapter Four

Land and Lawyers

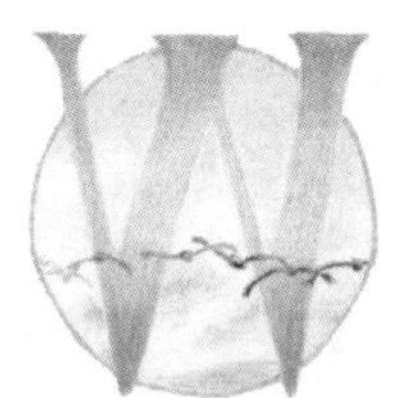

hen Hoffman purchased the large tracts of wild, thickly forested land on Bogue Banks from John A. Royall, although she had received a fee simple, or guaranty, title, which is "the highest and most complete ownership or enjoyment in real estate,"[215] she still had many legal difficulties with the property, perhaps of her making. As noted earlier, Hoffman had problems with the villagers of Salter Path who had lived in several different locations along the island for decades. After purchase of the property, Hoffman demanded that the villagers change their ways of living and abide by restrictions on their freedom. This, they refused to do. Hoffman knew they considered her an interloper, as two of the older inhabitants visited her and told her that as they had lived there for several generations, she should be satisfied with Shore House alone. Hoffman replied that she would not accede to their request, but would continue to allow them to remain on her land upon her conditions. She prohibited them from hunting, grazing livestock, fishing, or cutting fire wood from all her property, except within the village confines. As Salter Path measured one mile by approximately six hundred fifty feet, the villagers, by necessity, continued these activities on Hoffman's proscriptive property. Hoffman complained:

> The climax came one day when I laid out a new garden in strawberries. . . . The following morning I visited the spot . . . Not a vestige of a leaf was to be seen, & in place of the neat beds, & well defined alleys, only the marks of countless hoofs which had effaced all signs of the advance toward civilization.
>
> I began to investigate my rights in the matter & learned that one's title is supposed to invest one with an elusive tranquility called 'peaceful possession'. It occurred to me that the person who sold me the property would be the one to provide the above & as I could not be said ever to have had it, I laid my plans to acquire it without more delay.[216]

Hoffman wrote and requested Royall to have the Salter Path residents evicted, but he failed to reply to her letter. She then instructed her Beaufort attorney, Julius Duncan, to put pressure on Royall to do so. Duncan also refused to attend to the matter, for which Hoffman reproached him. Duncan replied, "The deputy [sheriff] suggested to me, having heard it in the neighborhood, at Salter Path [that] they will neither 'move' nor 'pay rentals.'"[217]

Hoffman repeatedly, but unsuccessfully, tried to have the people of the fishing community removed from her property. Many times, she notified the sheriff's office in Beaufort of some infringement on her property rights, but the deputies could never locate the trespassers. The villagers retained the legal services of Claude Wheatly, Beaufort attorney, in two separate suits against Hoffman. The first one was the attempt by David John Willis, representative of the entire community, to establish ownership by adverse possession. The second was an attempt to have their portion of Hoffman's land incorporated into a town, but the measure failed to pass the legislature.

Besides hunting and fishing on Hoffman's property and allowing their cattle and hogs to graze there, often, when Hoffman resided at her farm on Bogue Banks, the men of Salter Path would harass her and her employees, disturbing her by beating on pots and frightening her by chanting and shooting off guns close to her house. Finally, Hoffman decided to bring a lawsuit against the Salter Path residents for trespassing. Although Royall warned her through her New York law firm, Satterlee and Canfield, that if she carried through with the suit, she "would never be able to live there again,"[218] Hoffman hired E.H. Gorham and O.H. Guion, both local attorneys from Beaufort, to represent her in court. Duncan was the attorney for Royall, also named in the suit, and Wheatly represented the Salter Path people.

The suit, *Alice Hoffman v. J.C. Lewis, et al*, named thirty-five men from the village as defendants. Tried in Superior Court, Beaufort, during the June term 1923, Judge Henry A. Grady ruled in Hoffman's favor, declaring her the legal owner of the property and the villagers trespassers. Hoffman wrote:

> It was all so entirely unsatisfactory. I had to get up at 5:30 in order to be there on time. I had nothing to eat until 1 o'ck [*sic*] which prevented my thinking of anything except of how hungry I was! I never used my wits once, & lost an opportunity of making a marvelous impression upon not only the Salter Pathers but on the opposing counsel as well.[219]

Hoffman, "jockeyed into giving them more than [she] wanted,"[220] listened as Judge Grady declared:

> the above named defendants, and each of them and their descendants [*sic*] under them, may so long as the full terms and provisions of this Order are complied with, use, occupy, and enjoy all that certain strip or tract of land, now termed Salter Path, with the buildings, Churches, Schools, gardens and enclosures . . . and said defendants may use, for fishing, so much of the beach of said lands . . . herein allotted defendants.[221]

In turn, the court ordered the defendants to abide by several stipulations: keep off Hoffman's property (other than Salter Path), stop interfering with the management of her estate, quit bothering her and her employees, and graze their cattle and hogs only to the west of their boundary. Hoffman wrote to Miss Curtis, "It was a bad bargain."[222] Within a month she typed, "My Superintendent has been told by one of the fishermen at Salter Path that they do not intend to pay any attention to the injunction of the Court."[223] Although Hoffman won the court case, she could not evict the people of Salter Path. Furthermore, included in the June judgment was the decision that "this judgment, is . . . final, and neither Plaintiff nor defendants will appeal therefrom . . . and that plaintiff recover of defendants no cost or damages in this this action."[224] Hoffman had to pay the court costs. In anger over Gorham's handling of the lawsuit, she wrote, "I have been in such a collapsed condition since I have been here that I came home from the last day in court the most absolutely dejected creature that the earth has ever contained."[225] The 1923 Judgment created, as far as the village was concerned, a closed, unique environment. All Salter Path people could use, occupy, and enjoy all Salter Path.

Hoffman decided to change tactics, as the court prohibited an appeal to the lawsuit. She attempted to persuade her New York lawyers to represent her in a suit against Royall rather than the villagers. As always, Hoffman believed Royall ultimately responsible for the property's clouded title. Because of it, she was unable to mortgage the property. Forced to allow the Salter Path residents the use of the village property with the fishing rights in order to prevent any appeal of the case by them, Hoffman believed that Royall should pay the court costs which amounted to five hundred and fifty dollars.[226] Furthermore, she thought the suit would have been unnecessary if Royall had dealt with her honestly in the first place.[227]

Hoffman figured that the value of the village property should be deducted from the price she and Royall had agreed upon. She could not now obtain a guaranteed deed, as she had to allow the Salter Path people the use of the village for their natural lives and also permit their descendants the use of it, thus clouding the title. Hoffman demanded Royall to lower the price or evict the Salter Path residents. She thought that "$6750 taken off of the total would make it very pleasant in view of other plans I have in mind in connection with this place. It is improving in value in leaps and bounds."[228]

In an attempt to force the Salter Path villagers to abide by the restrictions on them in the 1923 judgment, Hoffman had the boundaries of Salter Path surveyed and markers put down at her expense. These were destroyed the same day and never replaced. She also took several of the village inhabitants to court for trespassing, but never received the satisfaction she desired as the charges could never be proved or the court simply warned the defendants to stay off Hoffman's property.

Hoffman decided to move ahead with the suit against Royall, as she thought that "certainly there should be some redress for the purchaser of a valuable piece of property whose valuable rights are used by others than the owner to his detriment."[229] Hoffman wanted her title to the property cleared and asked for redress for the loss of fishing profits and wood cut and taken from her property by the villagers.

Hoffman's New York lawyers, after a complete analysis of the case *Alice Hoffman v. J.C. Lewis, et al*, tried to dissuade her from filing a court case against Royall. They advised her that the verdict actually vindicated Royall of any responsibility, as she had agreed to amend the original deed to allow the Salter Path people to occupy their portion of her property. Her attorneys were of the opinion that she had no right of action against Royall and that she should continue to prosecute the individuals of Salter Path if trespassing occurred. Hoffman had already tried this course of action.

Satterlee and Canfield in New York reluctantly represented Hoffman in the lawsuit on the positive advice of Gorham, her Beaufort attorney. The presiding judge found for the defendant on the following grounds, as outlined to Hoffman by Satterlee and Canfield:

1. That your granting certain rights to squatters was inconsistent with the action on your part against Royall;

2. That any damage on account of the fishing was a damage which you suffered by reason of the use of your beach property for landing fish. Neither of the witnesses whom you brought was able to qualify as to the rental value of the landing:
3. Judge McGoldrick was willing to take evidence as to the amount of wood misappropriated by the squatters. The witnesses could give no testimony as to the amount of the wood so taken. The failure to prove rental value and the quantity of wood necessitated a directed verdict for the defendant.[230]

Hoffman replied that, against her better judgment, the judge in the 1923 case "persuaded [her] to allow certain rights covering a definite area which were not in any sense of the word squatters' rights in exchange for the agreement that the verdict should not be appealed."[231] Hoffman's explanation did nothing to change the judge's verdict and the responsibility of payment of this second case's court costs again fell to her. In addition to court costs, she received a letter from Satterlee and Canfield which stated:

> You will recall that in your action against John Royall you filed a bond for $500 for the purpose of attaching Royall's money and commencing the action. You having been defeated in the action, the Aetna Casualty & Surety Company were compelled to pay the amount of the bond to the attorneys for Royall and look to you for reimbursement . . . Will you kindly advise us what you can do to make payment of the $500 in question.[232]

Hoffman, again against the wishes of her attorneys, decided to appeal her suit against Royall. The final appeal came before the North Carolina Superior Court in March 1934, eleven years after the original judgment. F.A. Daniels, presiding judge, ruled that "this action be and same is dismissed; and plaintiff will pay the unpaid costs."[233]

Trouble then arose for Hoffman from another source. A little over a week after the suit Hoffman brought against the Salter Path inhabitants, she received a letter from Henry K. Fort, the Philadelphian to whom Royall had sold the western portion of the island, although according to Hoffman he had given her the option of buying it before he offered it to anyone else. Fort wrote:

> I am concerned about the stock ranging on my property on the western end of Bogue Banks, as well as other trespassing and depredations and I am taking steps on it. My information leads me to believe that if we were to erect a fence along our dividing line we would cut the ground from under those who believe there is some virtue in the exemptions in the recently passed law.[234]

Fort's reference to grazing animals and trespassing was, of course, to the Salter Path people. He wanted Hoffman to pay half the expenses of building a fence on their adjoining property but she replied that, although interested in a solution, she did not think that a fence was an adequate deterrent. Hoffman also hated to part with her money, perhaps an additional reason for her reluctance to help Fort.

Determined to protect his uninhabited island end from a few grazing cattle, Fort decided to take the same Salter Path men to court for trespassing as had Hoffman. As owner of the land and because she had agreed to allow the villagers to remain on her property, Fort named Hoffman as a defendant in his charges. She saw a plot in the affair. Royall once more emerged in her mind as the villain:

> Mr. Royall, through his fence Fort, is suing me for possession of the Johnson place. As I think you know I made my last payment on Bogue Banks accompanied by the Sheriff, who, after I had obtained my deed, proceeded to take charge of the money which is now reposing in the Bank until Mr. Royal shows just cause why he should claim the entire amount I promised him when he has never given me or made any effort to give me 'peaceful possession'.[235]

Fort wanted to erect a few rental cottages on his property along the beach. Hoffman wrote, "I wish him joy of his project. I believe that the musquitoes [*sic*] will drive every one away & that some day I shall have the opportunity of buying the whole shooting match. In the mean time I am not worrying."[236]

As in the 1923 court case with Hoffman, the Salter Path residents, with attorney Luther Hamilton representing them, again claimed title to ten acres of Fort's property owing to adverse possession. This claim constituted a cloud on Fort's title which had to be cleared in order for him to improve his property.

In October 1925, Fort's lawsuit came before the court. J.C. Lewis [the identical J.C. Lewis named in Hoffman's 1923 case] testified that he had "been paying taxes on the land 40 or 42 years. . . . Refers to receipt for $5.00 from Sheriff Hancock. My father gave me the land in 1921."[237] Byrd Willis, of Salter Path, testified that he had "known lands about 25 years" and Sam W. Dixon agreed that "it's about like Byrd says: Know the land 30 years. . . . I never used the land; been on it looking for cattle."[238] Moody C. Lewis, son of J.C. Lewis, also testified that "people been recognizing it as Pap's land since I can remember until they bothered it. It's about like Byrd says: People do what they please on it; never paid anybody anything for it."[239]

The court found that Fort was the legal owner in fee simple of the property in question. After the decision, Hamilton, the Salter Path residents' attorney, again attempted to gain title of the land for them. Hamilton submitted papers to the judge presiding which declared:

> In the report of the examiner no reference is made to the deed dated 1881 under which these defendants claim title to the land described therein, and it appears that in arriving at his conclusion the examiner did not have before him or in his mind the instrument referred to, and therefore could not have given due weight and proper consideration to the claims of the defendants.[240]

The court, however, decided to uphold a deed dated January 20, 1900, which stated that Joseph R. Johnson purchased the tract in question from George W. Styron and his wife, Susan C. Styron. The Styrons in turn sold the land to Royall, who sold it to Fort.[241] The court ordered the defendants to remove their cattle from the acreage. How those Salter Path cattle did roam about!

In March 1926, Julius Duncan, Royall's (and oftentimes Hoffman's) attorney who represented Fort in the case, declared that three of the defendants, J.C. Lewis, Arthur Smith, and Dexter Smith, refused to surrender possession of the land except upon the sheriff's demand. The court then issued an order to the sheriff, which read:

"Now, therefore we do command you, the said Sheriff that, without delay, you put the said J.C. Lewis, Dexter Smith and Arthur Smith out of possession of said lands, and that you put Henry K. Fort, or his legal representative, into the immediate possession of said described premises."[242] The court ordered the defendants off Fort's property and warned them never to interfere with him or his representatives again.

Hoffman, summoned to appear in court during this trial, apparently did not do so as there remains no record of any testimony given by her. She blamed Royall for the sale of the property to Fort and considered the entire lawsuit a ploy by Royall to further encumber her property. Royall, however, replied to Hoffman's attorneys' queries:

> [he had] offered Mrs. Hoffman 300 acres . . . to the east . . . in exchange for an equal amount of acreage . . . to the west, which would have included in its boundary Salter Path thus removing her from any ownership of land embraced within the settlement . . . Mrs. Hoffman declined my offer to trade . . . I had . . . done everything humanly possible to assist her, appreciating the difficulties under which she was laboring in attempting to manage a property so large and so diversified as this.[243]

The residents of Salter Path continued to live unrestricted until 1979, when another civil suit involving the village took place.

Sorting out Hoffman's subsequent land problems in North Carolina is as confusing now as it was then. Contradictions and discrepancies abound and the further one searches, the greater the muddle. How did she keep it all straight? The answer is: She did not. She became involved in taxation issues, which finally bested her. To begin to try to clear up her affairs, some old ground must be covered. Hoffman sailed to France in the mid-1920s, taking up residence at her home in Suresnes, and she frequently corresponded with the manager of her farm and properties in Carteret County. During the lengthy period of time that she lived in France, with several excursions to the United States, Hoffman claimed that she issued checks to her lawyer, E.H. Gorham, for tax payments on her property. In 1928, however, she received a letter from the office of Thompson, Koss and Warren in New York City which read:

> Some one from Newport, North Carolina sent in to Mr. Judge's office a clipping from a local paper down there stating that a certain property would be sold for taxes in the Town of Beaufort Carteret County, North Carolina on July 2, 1928, and in the list was the following: Mrs. Alice Hoffman 293 acres Johnson land 578 acres Glover land Bal $2,020.39. Doubtless you know all about this but I thought you ought to have this information in any event.[244]

Hoffman failed to respond, perhaps involved as she was then in the squabble with the French government over her Parisian estate.

Five years later, included among letters, documents, bills, and telegrams is another letter to Hoffman from the New York law office advising her to pay the overdue taxes on her Bogue Banks property. Although Hoffman again failed to answer, she did give some consideration to Shore House at that time, for she wrote her insurance agent, instructing him not to reduce the amount of insurance she carried on her Bogue Banks home as "with all the desperadoes that there are just now, I think a fire would be the logical thing to hide a theft."[245]

Finally, with the arrival of a third letter in April 1933, which warned Hoffman that her taxes had not been paid on her North Carolina land, she left France for America and arrived in the United States in the early summer of 1933. Hoffman wrote: "I learn[ed] to my horror that Mr. Gorham, after having forged endorsements on the checks [sent] direct to him . . . had let me in for an extra debt of about $35,000."[246]

Hoffman learned that all her property was scheduled to be auctioned off on the local courthouse steps for the unpaid taxes. Writing as though Gorham bore the guilt, Hoffman noted that there was a "possibility that the bank here which endorsed Mr. Gorham's signatures will be obliged to refund the money, which he used in part for his own needs, the last two checks that he wrote, which left 13 cents balance in my Bogue Banks Farms account, were written for the interest on his mortgage and for the last payment on his life insurance."[247] Yet Hoffman could not have Gorham arrested for the alleged embezzlement; he had died February 24, 1933 of influenza.

During Gorham's illness and after his death, his brother, W.C. Gorham, undertook Hoffman's legal affairs. The overseer of her Bogue Banks property, probably E. Abbott at the time, believing that Gorham did not show sufficient acumen in attending to Hoffman's business, asked attorney Llewellyn Phillips, whom Hoffman earlier had as partner in the fishing venture, to act for her until her return from France.

Hoffman concluded that Phillips was the answer to her questioning "what all these lessons that Providence has been putting to me."[248] She thought that he was exceptionally intelligent, although limited because he had been raised in a small town, and that he could benefit from her sophistication. She wrote that "we have so much in common that my Summer has been very interesting and [they had] achieved certain things which appeared to be very remote."[249]

In 1933, Phillips, at Eleanor Roosevelt's request, intervened for Hoffman when her overseer, E. Abbott, sued her for an unpaid bonus of $4,000.00. The court found in Abbott's favor, Hoffman commenting, "tho' how it was calculated I was never able to grasp."[250] As payment, the court allowed Abbott to seize and sell some of Hoffman's personal property. So Hoffman would not lose these possessions, Phillips bought the property at the sale on January 22, 1934.

Hoffman had made her niece, Eleanor, executor of her estate in 1929; she already was heir to Hoffman's properties. Later, as problems continued to develop, Eleanor, deciding that she did not want to be named in the inheritance, asked Hoffman to leave everything to her four children, grandchildren of President Theodore Roosevelt. At that time Hoffman agreed, stating in a letter to her accountant: "I am absolutely convinced that one day those children will be grateful to have a place to go to when the rest of the world becomes over-populated, and no matter how tempting a price may be offered for North Carolina I want you to remember that the person who owns real estate owns something, whereas the person who owns security owns nothing but paper in case of a general panic."[251] In an apparent change of heart, however, Hoffman, "having received the impression that Mrs. Roosevelt would not undertake the inheritance under any conditions, agreed to let Mr Phillips have the usufruit [usufruct] after [her] death."[252]

Actually, Hoffman did much more than that. When Her Carteret County property was about to be foreclosed on for nonpayment of taxes, Hoffman allowed E.H. Gorham and J.K. Warren, county tax commissioners who held her deed, to convey the title to Phillips. Although the conveyance is recorded at the Register of Deeds office March 18, 1935, it must have been signed sometime before February 23, 1933, the date Gorham died.[253]

Hoffman sailed again to France, not to return to America until 1938. She left Phillips in charge of all her affairs, arranging to send him his fees periodically, as well as money needed for maintenance, taxes, interest, and other charges. In the summer of 1937, Eleanor received a letter from a Mr. McNeill of Washington, DC. McNeill explained that he had been a close friend of her father-in-law, President Theodore Roosevelt, and he thought it only right to let her know that there were problems in connection with the way that Phillips was managing Hoffman's Bogue Banks property. Eleanor's youngest son, Quentin Roosevelt, sent Hoffman copies of the court records that McNeill had copied "to prove the justification of the assertions which he made that [Hoffman's] interests were not properly cared for."[254] McNeill desired to remain incognito.

NcNeill had indeed discovered financial difficulties with Hoffman's Carteret County holdings, but they were not of the kind he had imagined. Rather than a question of Phillips's mismanagement, Hoffman's problems originated in New York City. While she remained in France, certain attorneys, accountants, and businessmen decided they would no longer send Hoffman bills, but took legal action against her.[255] This may have been the reason for Hoffman's generous gift of trusteeship of her North Carolina properties to Phillips.

Believing Hoffman to be in North Carolina, Louis H. Pink, acting for the Union Indemnity Company of New York City, had the Clerk of Court of Carteret County issue a summons for Hoffman's appearance in court by September 2, 1936. The summons stated:

> Hoffman is a non-resident of North Carolina and has removed, (or) is about to remove some of her property from the State, with intent to defraud her creditors, (or) has assigned, disposed of (or) secreted, (or) is about to assign, dispose of (or) secrete some of her property with intent to defraud her creditors. [256]

The sheriff of Carteret County was instructed to "attach and safely keep all of the property of the said Mrs. Alice Hoffman."[257] Of course, the sheriff could not issue the summons to Hoffman, but he did attach the lien to her land and possessions.

About this time, Hoffman lost her French estate to the government there and returned to New York City. Taking up residence in a hotel, Hoffman soon learned that certain persons were glad to have her back. Faced with untold numbers of creditors in New York, Hoffman wrote:

> process servers have hovered around the threshold of the front door, including one such man [who] managed to enter the sitting room [but] was not able to hand the service either to me [or] Gabrielle [Hoffman's companion], who fell upon him with fists so valiantly that he left . . . yelling for the police. . . . In the Spring Mr. Harben . . . insisted that I should leave town before they could possibly catch me, so that when I went to Bogue Banks . . . I was actually in the car and on the road at five o'clock in the morning.[258]

Upon arrival at Bogue Banks, Hoffman claimed she found that Phillips had completely neglected the estate. She called Phillips to task, whereupon he engaged two persons to examine the premises. Hoffman noted:

> Mr and Mrs Miner . . . found the main house remarkably well cared for, not a suspicion of dampness. No mention was made of outside conditions, nor of my bathroom, allowed to leak . . . No notice was taken of this.[259]

Changing her mind concerning Phillips's interest in her well-being, however, Hoffman fired him. For once she was without a lawyer and she now definitely needed one, for she soon discovered the Pink lien upon her property. In a conference with Phillips, Hoffman asked why he had permitted the lien. He explained that he had had no alternative but to allow the sheriff to attach the lien to the property and that he did not think the Union Indemnity Company could receive a clear title. Phillips added that he had attempted to prevent Hoffman's other creditors from making any further attempts to seize her possessions. Characteristically, Hoffman decided to bring suit against Phillips to regain her property. She tried to talk to Phillips personally, but stated that she "heard language that [she] didn't know existed."[260] Hoffman wrote that after the short interview with Phillips, she "felt like a bombed Spaniard."[261]

Phillips retained former North Carolina governor, J.C.B. Ehringhaus, as his representative in the case. When Hoffman "heard rumors" that Phillips declared he made extra money, not from money she had wired from France, but from fishing in Florida, she drove to Raleigh to "acquaint Mr Ehringhaus with various facts . . . & he himself is only half inclined to continue with the case."[262] Ehringhaus explained that, as Phillips's counsel, he could not act for her and that she would need another attorney. Hoffman wrote that "as there is not a chance in the world of securing any one unprejudiced in this land of utterly unprincipled politicians, I stand to be again the victim of my folly in allowing things to have gotten to such an impasse."[263]

Hoffman then had an inspiration and wrote to her cousin in Ohio, Mary Matthias, wife of Ohio Supreme Court justice, Edward Matthias, and asked her to send "one among the galaxy of her young legal lights, who would protect [her] interests."[264] She sent her second son, John Marshall Matthias, to North Carolina to assist Hoffman.[265] Upon Matthias's arrival in Carteret County to act for Hoffman in the lawsuit, Hoffman wrote:

> Ex Gov Ehr. was very much impressed to learn that right in the family I had a young attorney, member of the Legislature, whose father was on the Supreme Court. But the public decided that he & his wife had come to catch Phillips out wh. [*sic*] they were looking forward to, & must be [a] G man![266]

Hoffman declared that "my cousin is just the pleasant adversary that Phillips needs."[267] Once again ready to engage in legal battle, Hoffman wrote, "It is a very delicate situation, & consists of attack & counterattack. . . . Just now my old superintendent has learned of the death of a sister and has gone to Virginia leaving me the full responsibility of a household situated in the midst of a neighborhood of more or less blood-thirsty natives!"[268] Hoffman noted that on the court date "[she] arose at dawn & sat in front of the Court-house, (la femme fatale)."[269] By close of day, however, the court had found Phillips not guilty of fraud, but had made no final decision on the legal title to the property. After negotiations between Hoffman, Matthias, and Phillips, Phillips conveyed his title to Matthias, who was to act as trustee of the property for Hoffman's niece, Eleanor. The Pink lien, however, remained against the estate.[270]

Although her name was removed from the title to the island property, Hoffman retained an interest in the land because she was in actual possession. Dissatisfied with this arrangement, however, Hoffman began a campaign to recover the deed.

Hoffman made several emotional attempts to persuade Matthias to relinquish the property's trusteeship, the culminating letter stating: "THE PROPERTY OF WHICH YOU ARE TRUSTEE IS BEING RUINED. WHAT DO YOU INTEND TO DO ABOUT IT."[271] As this ploy failed, Hoffman wrote her cousin, Mary, Matthias's mother, that "John's usefulness [was] over and that she had difficulty . . . getting his attention."[272] In a later letter to Mary in 1941, in reference to guns placed along the dunes by the army's 244th Coast Artillery unit, Hoffman typed: "The blow has fallen & the property for which I had purchasers amounting to well over a hundred thousand, has disappeared over night . . . no one in their sane senses would . . . buy Ocean front, interspersed with cannon."[273] Hoffman exclaimed: "I am glad Mr. Wooten died before he witnessed this tragedy!"[274] Apparently, Mary Matthias refused to answer. In an attempt to secure her personal property against creditors, Hoffman incorporated as Bogue Banks, Inc. in 1940. The company, however, had no assets.[275]

Immediately after the 1939 court settlement, Hoffman began receiving notices from the tax office in Beaufort for nonpayment of back taxes, although she insisted throughout this period that she was sending money to Matthias in Ohio for taxes and other indebtedness. Carteret County issued proceedings to sell the Hoffman property for nonpayment of taxes back to 1927. The county included all persons having any claim to the land, including John L. Crump, successor to Louis H. Pink. Sold in two sections, the Alden Corporation of Columbus, Ohio, acquired the property "west of Yeupon [*sic*] Point and that located upon the mainland" on April 25, 1942, for $7,865.28."[276] The same corporation purchased the portion of the land "which lies East of Yeupon [*sic*]" on August 8, 1942, for $7,865.28. The court confirmed the sales and as a result, the Alden Corporation acquired title to all the Hoffman property in Carteret County.

Apparently discontented with only one case in court, it should come as no surprise to learn that Hoffman, at this time, learned of yet another problem. Up to the 1940s, the village of Salter Path could only be reached by boat, but in 1940 the Works Progress Administration began to employ many of the men of Salter Path to clear a slender stretch of forest for a road down the island from Atlantic Beach to Salter Path. After cutting and clearing, they used mules to pull logs which smoothed the sand and then spread crushed shell gathered from shallow parts across the sound. At the time, a Raleigh newspaper reporter wrote, "It [the road] is unpaved and follows a picturesque winding course through and over the dunes, along plains and through live oak thickets. As the road crosses instead of going around a dune, the top of the jungle-like and wind-beaten oaks resembles a huge and verdant magic carpet, floating through a sea of blue and green."[277] The same reporter noted that "at one time this year 72 of the 75 men living at Salter Path were employed by the WPA."[278]

Hoffman discovered a sign erected by the villagers which read that they were incorporating her private road, which she claimed had cost thousands of dollars to build, into the new highway. Hoffman complained to the highway commissioner in Kinston, North Carolina, that "since my return it [the road] has been used by double tire trucks which have cut it all to pieces. As a matter of fact, it is being completely destroyed so far as my personal comfort is concerned."[279] Hoffman wanted her private road left alone and decided, once again, to obtain a restraining order from the court to halt the progressing road work.

Hoffman needed a lawyer to compose the necessary order. By chance, she found another attorney whom she thought she could trust with this task. Hoffman's cook, a widow with two sons to educate, had persuaded Frank M. Wooten, Sr., a Greenville, North Carolina attorney, to try to place them in a naval school. Wooten visited this woman at Shore House and met Hoffman there. After she told him her tale of woe regarding the encroachment of the road on her property, Wooten promised to look into the matter and advise her on her on legal alternatives. Wooten died a short time later, but his son, attorney Frank M. Wooten Jr. accepted Hoffman as a client.

After a thorough investigation, Wooten wrote Hoffman that he believed the clearing of trees for the roadway could be stopped. He based his opinion on the following:

1. According to information Salters [*sic*] Path . . . consists of approximately twenty-nine families. That between that settlement and Atlantic Beach there is no building, therefore, there is no need for such invasion.
2. Bogue Banks from Atlantic Beach westward to its end . . . has a substantial growth of timber that should be preserved.
3. Your forest is the outstanding forest on the Atlantic Coast and is the last of virgin natural forest so should be preserved in the manner that you are endeavoring to preserve it.
4. Salter Path, the waterways and the Beach have served the needs of this settlement for more than two hundred years. During that time

> there has been no increase in population and therefore, no need to invade this natural forest with a modern highway such as seems to be in contemplation.[280]

Wooten advised Hoffman that because he was not familiar with the property and the legal status of her interest in it, he could be of no further help, but she rushed to retain Wooten's services for the handling of all her affairs and apparently informed him of the problems she had encountered with the land and other local attorneys.

Hoffman's niece wrote to her, questioning her decision to hire yet another lawyer. Roosevelt asked, "Do you think it advisable to change to Mr. Wooten? I suppose you do, otherwise you wouldn't be changing. I just want to suggest that in the past (Gorham, Phillips, Haaren, etc. etc.) you haven't always been fortunate in choosing a representative or a lawyer, and I would certainly advise you not to do anything in a hurry."[281]

Roosevelt also told her aunt that she did not want to appear on the deed for the Bogue Banks property and asked that Matthias be named trustee for her four children instead. Roosevelt wrote that "apparently Mr. W [Wooten] does not know the reasons why you had to have the property put in someone else's name. This reason still exists, so far as I know."[282] Roosevelt requested Wooten remove her name from the title. Matthias then became trustee for the Roosevelt children: Grace Roosevelt McMillan, Theodore Roosevelt III, Quentin Roosevelt, and Cornelius Van Schaak Roosevelt.

Hoffman continued the fight to again have complete control of her property, charging Matthias that from the time he became trustee of the Bogue Banks property, he had "borrowed money to prevent me from receiving the income which I am entitled to, ignored my letters, gone out of his way to prejudice my family, & generally done the very opposite of protecting my interests."[283]

Wooten advised Hoffman that she could choose between two courses of action to have her name restored to the property's title. She could request the four Roosevelt children to convey to her a deed with all their rights and interests in the land or she could purchase in her own name the tax certificate which represented delinquent taxes, the cash value of which was approximately $4,000. The payment of the certificate would allow her to buy back the property. Unable to raise the money for the tax certificate, she asked Eleanor to speak to her children on the subject. Eleanor replied:

> Would you please, when you want the children to act, ask them yourself? It takes just that much longer to write to me to write to them. Besides, they are all grown up men and women now, and I do not want the responsibility of requesting them to do anything as far as property is concerned. They are old enough to make up their own minds.[284]

In August, 1940, the four Roosevelt heirs issued Hoffman a quitclaim deed to the Bogue Banks property. With the knowledge that Hoffman was and had been in actual possession of the estate for twenty-five years, either personally or through her employees, they wanted to guarantee her a home. The deed stated:

> the heirs desire to release, discharge and quit-claim the said property unto the said party of the second part [Hoffman] in consideration of natural love and affection, which the parties of the first part bear to their great-aunt . . . in consideration of the parties of the first part being wholly relieved and discharged from all possible liability for delinquent taxes on said property and any and all other liability of every kind and nature which has attached to said property.[285]

Although Hoffman's great-niece and great-nephews issued this deed to her, Matthias, as trustee, also needed to relinquish his interest in the property. Wooten had examined the legal document which made Matthias trustee and found that it gave Matthias the right to sell a portion of the property to pay outstanding debts. Hoffman informed Eleanor that Matthias was "considering an offer from a person who is a member of the racing commission here, in other words a clique of gamblers who would be glad to obtain a plot of Beach front property & not only make two or three hundred % out of it, but introduce an element which I cannot accept as a neighbor!"[286] Hoffman acknowledged that she would have to have someone as trustee, due to her financial difficulties, and therefore decided "it would be best to let John [Matthias] continue, after the [document] is written over so that he is obliged to allow me to decide matters which he does not understand."[287]

In March, 1941, Matthias, as fiduciary for the Roosevelt children, relinquished his trusteeship and executed a quit-claim deed to Hoffman. The indenture stated:

> WHEREAS, Llewellyn Phillips, Trustee . . . and his wife . . . executed and delivered to [Matthias] that certain deed . . . erroneously representing that they owned the property therein described . . . and,
>
> WHEREAS, it now appears that the said deed above cited of Phillips is tainted with fraud, tending to affect the rights of A. Hoffman . . . It now appearing that A. Hoffman was the actual owner of the property described in said deed, and
>
> WHEREAS, [Matthias] was not fully advised as to the purpose and intent of said Phillips did inadvertently and without full information concerning the same receive said deed of said Phillips . . . and,
>
> WHEREAS, [Matthias] for the purpose of correcting his own error in inadvertently accepting said deed of Phillips, does execute this quit-claim deed, hereby demonstrating his good faith.[288]

Hoffman's name was returned to the title with Matthias continuing to act as trustee. The deed, however, remained clouded with several people claiming some interest in the property. Also, and more importantly, the taxes on the estate had still not been paid to the county. Again, the property was foreclosed upon for nonpayment of taxes.

Wooten decided that a complete analysis of title to the property would be necessary if he was to renew any action on Hoffman's part. Researchers traced the ownership of the Bogue Banks property to Christopher Gale, chief justice of the province of North Carolina. On March 30, 1720, the title to the entire island, then known as Borden Banks, was granted to Gale for £76. The subsequent ownership revolved around two conflicting claims. From that date until 1866, the transfers of island property are vague and involved among the descendants of Gale and William Borden. Gale and Borden both conveyed the title to their respective children. The county records do not show all the transfers or even continuity of transfers. After completion of the title search, Wooten wrote Hoffman that he considered the deed granted to the Alden Corporation void and advised her to institute an action to remove cloud from the title. Wooten, in reference to the deed granted to Phillips, wrote Hoffman that the deed appeared void as it was executed "for the purpose of obstructing, hindering and delaying creditors holding claims against you."[289] Wooten also advised Hoffman:

> You have been in adverse possession of Bogue Banks under known and visible lines and boundaries for more than twenty years . . . I advise you to institute action to remove cloud from title, and proceed with plans to pay delinquent taxes and judgment debts. . . . you would be asserting your title by possession against the deeds, which in my opinion are void, and proceed to assert your objection to the construction of the road through your property, which is objectionable to you.[290]

Hoffman decided to pursue another course of action. With Wooten now her legal representative, Hoffman brought a lawsuit against Matthias, Phillips, and the Alden Corporation for fraud. She claimed that they had conspired to obtain title to the property for their own gain and had made a definite and determined effort to deprive her of her home. Hoffman asked for sole ownership of the land, the cloud removed from title, and exclusive fishing rights. Hoffman also stated that she no longer wished to leave the property to the Roosevelt children after her death, but wanted it conveyed to the state of North Carolina.

Matthias, with Columbus, Ohio, attorney J. Paul McNamara as his counsel, had to return to North Carolina for the fifth and final hearing on Hoffman's Bogue Banks property, held in a special civil court session in August 1944. Hoffman was eighty-two years old. The court found Matthias, Phillips, and the Alden Corporation not guilty of fraud, but ordered the following provisions:

> 1. Mrs. Alice Hoffman to have irrevocable license to use all of the property except two mile area adjacent to Atlantic Beach.
> 2. That John Marshall Matthias, as Trustee for Roosevelts, holds option to purchase land from Alden. That so much of excepted areas as necessary be sold to clear indebtedness of property and other necessary expenses of the trust. That none of these sales to interfere with use of property by Mrs. Hoffman.
> 3. The outstanding fishing lease to prevail for years 1944, 1945 and 1946, rental basis being two shares.

4. Mrs. Hoffman to have income from fishing rights after payment of taxes on the property.[291]

Lastly, it was ordered that "Mrs. Alice Hoffman [is] to have no further interest therein."[292]

A deed conveyed by the Alden Corporation on June 8, 1945, to Matthias, trustee for the Roosevelts, conveyed all Hoffman's property on Bogue Banks and the mainland to the Roosevelts. Another court decision on the land came on February 2, 1948, when Wachovia bank was named trustee of the property for the children of Eleanor Butler Roosevelt. Other than the land, the assets of the trust amounted to $3,500.00. This judgment stated that "Mrs. Hoffman has a license to live upon the property."[293]

On July 15, 1950, John Marshall Matthias resigned his trusteeship of the Hoffman land and Theodore Roosevelt III was appointed trustee.[294]

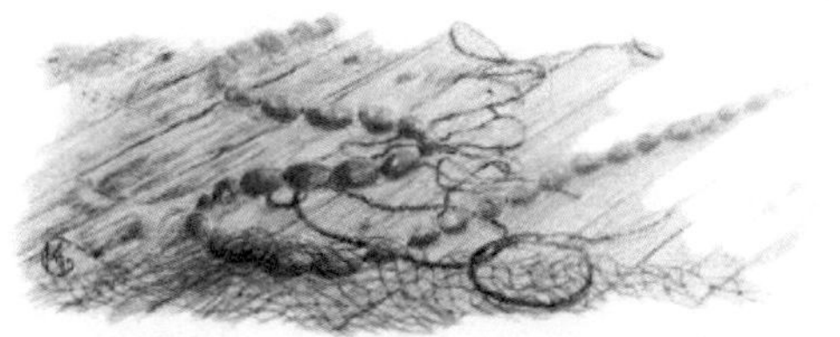

Chapter Five

Queen Alice

lice Hoffman died on March 15, 1953 at Shore House on Bogue Banks. She was buried in the family plot in Greenwood Cemetery in New York City. *The Carteret County News-Times* obituary notice listed her survivors as Mrs. Theodore Roosevelt, Jr., daughter-in-law of the late president, and Hoffman's companion, Gabrielle Brard. Erroneously, the notice stated that her father, Albert Green, served one term as New Jersey governor. The article also noted that "some years ago, Mrs. Hoffman signed her property over to a trust naming John Marshall Matthias, an Ohio judge, as trustee."[295]

During her lifetime, Hoffman did indeed work to "be somebody." Perhaps, truly, she wished to be a queen. Her great-niece, Alexandra Roosevelt Dworkin, Eleanor's granddaughter, recalled hearing her described as "extravagant, neglectful of debts, and pampered."[296] Dworkin noted that Hoffman, in the manner of royalty, "never dressed herself, but always employed a maid or companion to do so."[297]

Hoffman's cousin, Alice Jacoby [named for Hoffman], likewise remembered that "Aunt Alice wanted everything done for her."[298] Jacoby stated that once, as she and her sister, Florence Merkel, stopped to visit Hoffman at a hotel in Washington, DC, she refused them entrance to her rooms, explaining that her maid, Gabby, was busy, organizing Hoffman's clothes. Jacoby stated: "She [Hoffman] brought a straight-backed chair into the hall where we waited and sat on it just like a queen"[299] as they talked.

The irony is that Alice Hoffman was a queen, had she recognized and appreciated her kingdom and chosen to wear its crown; she was "The Queen of Bogue Banks." "Monarch of all she surveyed," she could have been Defender of her portion of a rare barrier island, Protector of its intrinsic beauty, and Governor of her fishing village. Imagine half of Bogue Banks as perhaps the Hoffman Preserve, in its natural state, thickly forested, wild, free, its land, marshes, shores, beaches, and waters teeming with life, and possibly caretakers from within the Salter Path community. But, she did not so choose.

Hoffman spent long years in the attempt, as she stated, "not . . . to lose any portion of what I have accumulated if it could be avoided."[300] Apparently, she squandered money on herself early in life. Overseas travel was expensive, and especially so if one demanded the best of everything.

By the time Hoffman began her investments in New York City, she decided she needed more money to live than she received from her inheritances. Hoffman asked William Kingsley, President of the United States Trust Company, for more money immediately after buying the building at 17 East 54th Street, which held a penthouse apartment:

> You were kind enough to lend me the money which I needed to close the title. Subsequent events in France . . . compelled me to furnish the house (for which you very generously advanced me a further amount) and get an income out of it . . . Mrs. Alexander [Hoffman's sister] . . . has kindly placed some of her collateral at my disposal, which has saved the situation temporarily . . . I have no-one else to appeal to and cannot but feel that you do not understand the situation. [301]

Kingsley relented, for at the bottom of the letter, Hoffman typed: "Mortgage increased upon my promise not to ask for further accommodation."[302]

Recalling the New York City slums, one wonders about the condition of some of Hoffman's buildings there. In the same letter to Kingsley, Hoffman stated that in 1927, she had received a letter from a J. Thorpe that he intended to demolish one of the buildings she had sold him. Concerning the rents she received on the buildings, she thought that as America was not very prosperous during those years, and although she obtained a higher rent, her tenants were frequently unsuccessful and hat to be replaced.

As noted, Hoffman refused or neglected to pay her many retainers, constantly squabbling, or simply ignoring them. Thus, Hoffman often changed attorneys, overseers, accountants, servants, and others. Even Gabrielle Brard, her companion of twenty-two years, threatened to quit her service owing to low wages.[303]

As to Hoffman's love of her North Carolina home, until 1938 she seldom resided there, preferring France or New York City. Having established Pine Grove Farms on Bogue Banks, she left its management to others, remaining absent for years on end. Finally, after leaving France and fleeing before creditors from New York City, Hoffman decided to remain on Bogue Banks.

Always looking for a money-making enterprise in North Carolina, Hoffman several times called in experts to survey the property and calculate the value of the timber. Throughout the time of her lawsuits with Phillips and Matthias, Hoffman attempted to raise money from selling timber. She received letters from both John Royall and his wife, Agatha, concerned about the destruction of trees on her island property. Royall denounced Hoffman, stating that he had refused to sell the property to others because of their intent to carelessly develop it.

Hoffman never befriended the Salter Path villagers and often ridiculed them. In a letter to Sam Duplanty, she wrote: "It is too bad about S.P. people. It is a mystery that they are not all sick, all of the time, the way they live. Do be careful not to allow them to walk about. The first thing we know the place will be infected with hookworm."[304] Even as several Salter Path men and women worked intermittently at Shore House, Hoffman schemed against them. In 1941, she wrote Mary Matthias:

> The judgment proving my title in 1923 made it a misdemeanor for anyone to enter for any reason whatever on my land and was brought against the thirty [actually thirty-five] members of the Village of Salter Path who claimed squatter's rights. A notice in the paper recently says that the village will have forty-five subscribers to the new electrical installation. This will mean a great deal of legal work to prove that out of the original thirty, of whom fifteen have died, the other thirty must be requested to move away. I do not propose to allow [them] to live on my land without paying rent or taxes. I wouldn't let them stay even if they paid both.[305]

In yet another and vastly different way to raise money, on February 9, 1944, Hoffman wrote to publisher Alfred A. Knopf regarding the likelihood of publication of her autobiography. Herbert Weinstock, representative of the publishing house, answered:

> I see no reason, to judge from the description you give of your manuscript, to believe that it would not be suitable as a contestant for one of the Alfred A. Knopf Fellowships for 1944—the biography fellowship. The autobiography of an American would certainly fit into the scheme.[306]

She requested a fellowship application from the publishing house, stating:

> I was born in New York, & have been over a great part of the world, owing to the fact that since I was 21 I have been financially independent, & divided my time between my home in Paris, New York & North Carolina . . . Just now I am in my property in N.C. . . . more or less free to devote myself to finishing my book. . . . I enclose an early photograph of the author, at the age of two. There are many more recent ones.[307]

Herbert Weinstock, for the publishing company, answered Hoffman that from the description of the manuscript, perhaps she could become a contestant for the Alfred A. Knopf Fellowship for 1944. Hoffman sent the unfinished autobiography which contained the following chapters: "Racing in Paris; A Summer in Southampton; A Visit in Pekin [*sic*] with the English Ambassador's Wife, and A Winter in Sweden at the Suggestion of Mme. de Hermann Lindecrone." Apparently, having read the rambling, pretentious account, Bernard Smith replied for the publication firm that, regretfully, they could not offer Hoffman an award or any other publishing proposals.

Fragments of sentences from just two of Hoffman's many letters serve to adequately describe her: "Contrived to get possession of it; compelled to move; rumors which have circulated that I am ruined and unable to pay my debts; unjustified claim of an unpaid light bill; Mr. Gorham hoodwinked Mr. Judge; my property, which is coveted by all and sundry; foreclosed illegally; money which they have taken that belonged to me; what I require to live in a carefree manner; it is not my fault."[308]

It is difficult, however, and perhaps unfair to look at a lifespan of ninety years and pronounce absolute judgment on it. Did Hoffman manipulate others based on societal place, money, or connection to the Roosevelts? Was she entirely self-serving? Did others take advantage of her as a woman, a foreigner, a Northerner? Why did she spend most of her life in strife? What happened after the travel and dancing and horse-racing were over? I go back to stories and opinions about her from people here who either remember her or know those who do. I hear that she was a good, caring person who loved Bogue Banks, an early conservationist. I hear that she was a selfish, greedy person who would have cut down every tree on the island for a decent price and confiscated all the fish caught. Who *was* Alice Hoffman?

On February 25, 1949, those with an interest in the Bogue Banks property, including Hoffman, Matthias, and Eleanor's four children, the Roosevelt heirs, issued a deed to a portion of the property to the Reverend Thomas H. Wright, Bishop of the Diocese of Eastern North Carolina, also H.C. Rorison and Robert Strange, trustees for the diocese. After Hoffman's death in 1953, the Roosevelt heirs conveyed title of a second portion of the island land to the State of North Carolina. The remainder of the property, except for another gift to the state on June 3, 1980, was developed into business and residential areas, including houses and condominiums.

Left was Salter Path. Heirs of the thirty-five men named on the 1923 judgment still lived in the village. As the Roosevelt heirs had stopped paying taxes on the property and the villagers did not own the land to pay taxes, in 1979 Carteret County filed a suit against the Roosevelts and the inhabitants of the village for nonpayment.

During the civil suit, which many believe was the beginning of the end for the unity and uniqueness of the village, each head of household in Salter Path was required to trace his or her ancestry to at least one of the original thirty-five men named in the 1923 judgment. Three families could not, and were given two years to move from the village. All others laid claim to their individual plots of land, paid the court costs and seven years back taxes on personal property, and were issued deeds by the Roosevelt heirs.

The judge presiding, Robert Rouse, remarked, "That 120 separate pieces of property were surveyed for ownership and deeds, with only two minor disputes, testifies to the character of the Salter Path villagers and the unity among them."[309]

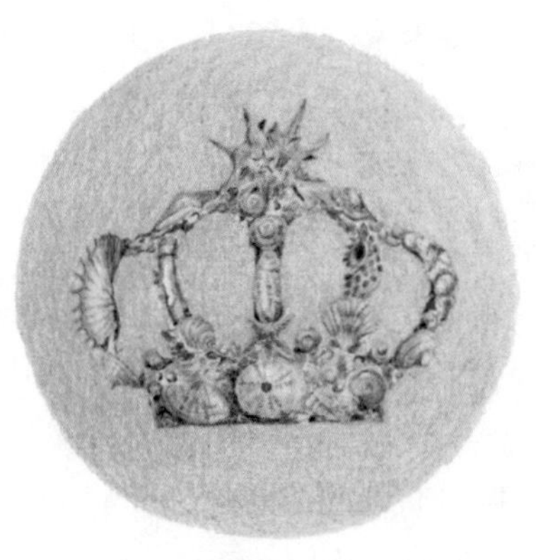

Conclusion

o I come to the end of the story in 1979, but it's not the end because that was some time ago. Have the years been blank? Of course not. As to me, I'm older, but still in the same place with the same husband. Shore House was torn down, and other homes sit on Hoffman's property in a place now called Pine Knoll Shores. Hoffman's heirs, the four grandchildren of President Theodore Roosevelt, have died. Most of the people in my account are gone. Bogue Banks has changed beyond belief, well, no, if I look around, I find I must believe. If I could write like Rick Bragg, I'd write a conclusion that would make you weep, but I'm not Rick Bragg and this is not his story.

Alice Hoffman, in bringing a case of eviction to court in 1923, changed, but did not yet destroy, Salter Path. Before then, people here were isolated and free, moving in rhythm with the tides and the seasons. No bridge, no ferry crossed Bogue Sound, and no road led to the settlement. As Ben MacNeill wrote in 1926:

> How they came to settle here nobody remembers, but like all the people who live along these banks, they must have come to fish. Or perhaps they just came, and since fishing was all that offered them the means of living, they fished. They have fished for two centuries . . . Ownership of land seems not to have occurred to them. They came here 200 years ago as there was none who claimed any land on the banks. Only those hardy enough to live on it. There was none to claim it, and none did claim it, save these men who lived on it. It was theirs, because none told them they could not use it, and they have possessed it through the years.[310]

From 1923 until 1979, Salter Path people fared well, part of the land and water. They worked in commercial fishing as they scalloped, shrimped, set crab-pots, gill-netted, long-hauled, fished on the beach, and did anything they could do in between—clammed, picked up oysters, conched, scooped soft crabs. Everyone worked together and worked hard. No one had much, but people had fun. As time went on, Salter Path had its own school, stores, churches, a theater, a filling station, a small restaurant. They founded a volunteer rescue squad and fire department. (Oh, you should hear the stories about them.) Salter Path folks built a ballfield here! Men played baseball around the county on Salter Path teams, and women played softball. Men hunted, choirs sang in the churches, children played in the evenings, kids learned to surf in the '60s, and people got together in fish houses or on porches. Holding up everything, at the center of everything, was work. Through all those years, Salter Path remained closed, isolated, and unique. (I can hear people say, "What, all the way out there? There's only Salter Pathers out there.) No one could move in; not many moved out. Most here are related: Willis, Guthrie, Salter, Frost, Lewis, Pittman, Smith, and a few others. People from Salter Path felt at home here and no matter where they went, they just had to get back to that tiny place between the ocean and the sound, and everything was okay. Salter Path folks remained different, talked differently, thought differently. Everyone knew everyone else; every home was open.

But the 1923 judgment was still in effect, although no one much thought about it. Up in New York and New Jersey, the Roosevelts, Alice Hoffman's heirs, decided they needed to shake things up in Salter Path. In 1979, Salter Path was surveyed, measured, divided up, and, for the first time, owned by many individuals. As people here married, they could no longer clear a place and start a home. No room was left. People discovered Bogue Banks, and as they began to build vacation homes, second homes, and rental houses, Salter Path land became valuable, so little by little, some here sold their homes, until today approximately a third of Salter Path is owned by others. Taxes increased, insurance costs soared, and tourism invaded. A few preferred to live elsewhere. Commercial fishing decreased and began dying. David Ivester, of James Styron's Fish Co. said on March 28, 2010: "This is the last generation of fishermen in Carteret County."[311]

And so, Alice Hoffman changed the world, our world. What happens if people are a part of a place? With roots there, just like a tree? What do they do if the root system is damaged? Yearn, that's what. Author Barbara Allen wrote that "a sense of place, a consciousness of one's physical surroundings, is a fundamental human experience."[312] Salter Path folks' attachment to home, no matter where they live—their sense of place in history—is their identity.

A crowd of Salter Path men fished on the beach for mullet this past fall, as they had when the Roosevelt heirs owned the land, when Alice Hoffman owned the land, when John Royall owned the land, when no one wanted the land. They had a pretty good season. But next year? And the next? On the beach one day, while they cleared the net of mullet, a man from somewhere interviewed Henry Frost about beach fishing. Henry, the eighty-one year old owner of Frost Fishing Crew, after answering many questions, finally told him: "Right now I've got my sons and my grandsons here fishing, but I'm looking for my home, and I can't seem to find it."

Endnotes

Chapter One

[1] Ethel C. Phillips, "Woman of Mystery - Alice Grene [sic] Hoffman," *The Heritage of Carteret County North Carolina Vol. I*, 1982, 385.
[2] William A. Link and Arthur S. Link, *American Epoch: A History of the United States Since 1900, Volume I: War, Reform, and Society 1900-1945* (New York: McGraw-Hill, Inc., 1993), 77.
[3] Hoffman autobiography. Typewritten manuscript, Alice Green Hoffman Papers, Collection No. 127, East Carolina Manuscript Collection, J.Y. Joyner Library, East Carolina University, Greenville, NC.
[4] E. Idell Zeisloft, quoted in Grace Mayor, *Once upon a City* (New York: The Macmillan Company, 1958), 114.
[5] "[Theodore Roosevelt, Jr.] was married in New York city [*sic*], June 20, 1910, to Eleanor Butler, daughter of Henry Addison Alexander of that city, a lawyer, and had four children." *National Cyclopaedia of American Biography* (New York: J.T. White and Company, 1891 [first publication]), 613f. Hoffman's niece, Eleanor, wife of President Theodore Roosevelt's son, Theodore Roosevelt Jr., should not be confused with Franklin Delano Roosevelt's wife, Eleanor.
[6] Mary Frances Crouch Green to Grace Green, 28 August 1864, Hoffman Papers.
[7] Hoffman autobiography.
[8] Ibid.
[9] Marilyn French, introduction to *Roman Fever and Other Stories*, by Edith Wharton (New York: Berkeley Books, 1981), viii.
[10] Hoffman autobiography.
[11] Ibid. Oddly, Hoffman much later recalled that the man wore a Civil War uniform and that he died shortly afterward in an accident while duck hunting.
[12] Ibid. John E. Matthias, Hoffman's distant cousin, recalled that Hoffman discovered before the wedding that her fiancé was quite a libertine. Embarrassed, however, to cancel the large ceremony to be held in Paris, Hoffman played the part of bride and then immediately filed for divorce. Matthias hesitated to state that his recollection was entirely correct. J. Paul McNamara, attorney for the Matthias family, corroborated the story and added that he thought more than likely the marriage was never consummated. John E. Matthias and J. Paul McNamara, interview by author, telephone, 19 April 1994.
[13] Ibid. Hoffman penned in a margin of her autobiography, "Ellis's phil[osophy] of life being that what you don't know won't hurt you."

[14] William H. Clarke to Alice Hoffman, 23 December 1919 and Schedules A and B, receipts of income from October 1, 1928 to October 1, 1929, Hoffman Papers. The buildings were located at 137-9 Wooster Street, 267 West Broadway, 57-9 East 117th Street, and 433 Fifth Avenue. The mills included Darlington Manufacturing Co., Darlington, SC; Monarch Cotton Mills, Union, SC; Laurens Cotton Mills Company, Spartan Mills, Pacolet Manufacturing Company, all of Spartansburg, SC; Dolls Manufacturing Company, Huntsville, AL; Gainsville Cotton Mills, Gainsville, AL; Dallas Manufacturing Company, Dallas, TX. Theron Butler joined many other Northerners in investment in the South. C. Vann Woodward noted that in the South "a widespread practice was to raise only part of the required capital locally and then issue a large percentage of the stock of a new [cotton] mill to Northern . . . firms." C. Vann Woodward, *Origins of the New South* (Baton Rouge: Louisiana State University Press, 1971), 135.

[15] Hoffman wrote that "to return from my first European visit without any clothes seemed to me unthinkable." Hoffman autobiography.

[16] Ibid. Hoffman mistakenly referred to a fictional von Munchausen, although a real Baron Hieronymus Karl Friedrich Munchasen lived in Germany in the 1700s.

[17] Ibid.

[18] Ibid.

[19] Ibid.

[20] Ibid.

[21] Ibid. Because of stitches and black eyes, Hoffman avoided company for several weeks after the accident.

[22] Ibid.

[23] "Following his [Theodore Roosevelt, Jr.] graduation at Harvard University he spent two years as a wool sorter in the mill of the Hartford Carpet Co. at Thompsonville, Conn., and during 1910-12 was manager of the company's distributing branch in San Francisco, Calif. He then went to New York city [*sic*] and served as a bond salesman with Bertron, Griscom & Jenks during 1912-14." At age fifty-six, Roosevelt was the only general to land with the first wave of troops on D-Day, June 6, 1944. He led the assault and commanded operations on Utah Beach, winning the Medal of Honor. His son Quentin Roosevelt was in the first wave to land on Omaha Beach. Theodore Roosevelt Jr. died of a heart attack on July 12, 1944 near Sainte-Mire-Eglise. He is buried in the American World War II Cemetery in Normandy. *National Cyclopaedia*, 612.

[24] M.C. Clark to United States Engineering Office, 20 May 1920; Jamaica Hillcrest Company to Alice Hoffman, 1 June 1921.

[25] William G. Green to Alice Hoffman, 27 February 1920, Hoffman Papers.

[26] Alice Hoffman to Herbert L. Satterlee, 22 December 1928, Hoffman Papers.

[27] The lawsuit remained on the court docket for eight years, as the court continually granted Fraad a recess.

[28] William Dutka to Alice Hoffman, 19 November 1929, Hoffman Papers.

[29] Alice Hoffman to William Kingsley, Hoffman Papers.

[30] Ida H. Buck to Alice Hoffman, 20 May 1931, Hoffman Papers.

[31] Alice Hoffman to Herbert Satterlee, 18 December 1928, Hoffman Papers.

[32] Herbert Satterlee to Alice Hoffman, 18 February 1929, Hoffman Papers.
[33] Hoffman's papers include many financial statements, although one may give an idea of Hoffman's financial worth throughout a number of years. In 1908, inventories of the Theron R. Butler Trust, including real estate, stocks, bonds, interest on mortgages and bank balances, and rents, showed a value of $1,941,646.25. Eleven years later, in 1918, the same inventories showed that the value had decreased to $125,696.98. Hoffman handled her own financial affairs. Although she attempted to hold on to her money, some mismanagement occurred to cause this decline. William H. Clarke, CPA, to Alice Hoffman, TLS, 23 December 1919.
[34] Actually, by this time, Hoffman had several mortgages on the building. Alice Hoffman to Llewellyn Phillips, 1 January 1938, Hoffman Papers.
[35] Hoffman autobiography.
[36] Maggie Duplanty to Alice Hoffman, 7 December 1923, Hoffman Papers.
[37] Egbert's humor was lost on Hoffman, however, as subsequent bills from the company took on a much more serious note.
[38] Hoffman autobiography.
[39] Alice Hoffman to Charles E. Lauriat, 10 January 1929, Hoffman Papers.
[40] Hoffman autobiography.
[41] Ibid.
[42] Ibid.
[43] Ibid.
[44] Ibid.
[45] Ibid.
[46] Ibid.
[47] Ibid.
[48] "In 1929 Herbert Hoover, then President, appointed [Theodore] Roosevelt [Jr.] civil governor of Puerto Rico. In 1932 Hoover appointed him governor general of the Philippines." *National Cyclopaedia*, 612.
[49] Williamson Pell to Alice Hoffman, 19 January 1931, Hoffman Papers.
[50] Hoffman autobiography.
[51] Ibid.
[52] Ibid.
[53] Ibid.
[54] Ibid.
[55] Ibid.
[56] Alice Hoffman to William Kingsley, 9 November 1929, Hoffman Papers.
[57] Hoffman autobiography.
[58] Ibid. Hoffman, with characteristic paranoia, stated that "the Front Populaire, which had recently overthrown [the existing government], not constitutionally, but through another political ruse, decided that they would like to acquire my one ewe lamb by dispossession, for the feeble pretext of 'Public Utility.' It had been for sale before for twenty years before I found it, but the very fact that I owned it made it seem desirable above all else."

[59] Alice Hoffman to Llewellyn Phillips, 27 January 1936; and Hoffman autobiography.
[60] Hoffman autobiography.
[61] Alice Hoffman to Herbert Satterlee, 18 December 1928, Hoffman Papers.
[62] Alice Hoffman to Eleanor Roosevelt, 13 November 1928, Hoffman Papers.
[63] Ibid.
[64] Hoffman autobiography.
[65] Ibid.
[66] Alice Hoffman to S.S. Szlapka, 25 November 1938, Hoffman Papers.
[67] William Kingsley to Alice Hoffman, 8 November 1929, Hoffman Papers.
[68] Lester D. Egbert to Alice Hoffman, 21 July 1930, Hoffman Papers.
[69] Alice Hoffman to Raymond Harper, 28 July 1938, Hoffman Papers.
[70] Alice Hoffman to Eleanor Roosevelt, 13 November 1928, Hoffman Papers.
[71] Alice Hoffman to Raymond Harper, 27 October 1938, Hoffman Papers.
[72] Hoffman autobiography.
[73] Ibid.

Chapter Two

[74] Hoffman autobiography.
[75] Another story of Hoffman's discovery of the North Carolina property, told to the author by Alexandra Roosevelt Dworkin, Hoffman's great-great-niece, is that Hoffman was riding on a train from New York to Florida when she overheard two men talking of a beautiful, isolated piece of property in Carteret County, NC. One of the men was on his way to buy it. Hoffman got off the train in Morehead City in Carteret County and immediately put a down-payment on the Bogue Banks land. Although Hoffman rode to Florida on a train, the train would not have passed through Morehead City. Hoffman herself related the story of the advertisement in the paper, which seems more plausible. Alexandra Dworkin, interview by author, telephone, 9 February 1994.
[76] David Bertelson, *The Lazy South* (New York: Oxford University Press, 1967), 58f.
[77] Ibid., 180, 240.
[78] Walter Hines Page, 4 February 1886, quoted in Lindley S. Butler and Alan D. Watson, eds., *The North Carolina Experience: An Interpretive and Documentary History* (Chapel Hill, NC, 1984), 330.
[79] Woodward, *Origins of New South*, 406.
[80] Mrs. Fred Hill, ed., *Historic Carteret County North Carolina*, 103f.
[81] Ibid., 103.
[82] Ibid.
[83] Ibid.
[84] Ibid.
[85] Tony P. Wrenn, *Beaufort, North Carolina* (Falls Church, Va.: EconoPrint, 1970), 8f.
[86] Hoffman autobiography.
[87] Ibid.
[88] Ibid.
[89] S.P. Hancock to Alice Hoffman, 28 June 1917, Hoffman Papers.

[90] Hoffman autobiography.
[91] Alice Hoffman to Lester D. Egbert, 11 July 1933, Hoffman Papers.
[92] Michael B. Alford, "A Look at the Historical Watercraft of Carteret County," Davis and Hamilton, eds., *Heritage of Carteret County*, 35.
[93] Hoffman autobiography.
[94] Ibid.
[95] Ibid.
[96] Ibid.
[97] Ibid.
[98] Ibid.
[99] Ibid.
[100] James C. Cobb, "Why Southern Industrialization Hasn't Worked That Way," quoted in Paul D. Escott and David R. Goldfield, eds., *Major Problems in the History of the American South, Volume II: The New South* (Lexington, Mass., 1990), 536.
[101] Cindy Tugman, "Life in Morehead City," Davis and Hamilton, eds., *Heritage of Carteret County*, 117.
In 1918, 2,708 persons were engaged in fishing in Carteret County with a total investment of $1,475,828. Total seafood catches in the county in pounds and dollar values were as follows: Menhaden, 90,232,799, $480,212; Mullet, 428,355, $23,804; all other fish, 7,339,324, $246,312; Crabs, 225,665, $23,961; Clams, 47,176. $8,103; Oysters, 879,977. $31,925; Scallops, 415,572. $30,768. A. Lefferts, H.C. Lay, C.W. Lewis, *UNC Extension Bulletin* (Chapel Hill, NC: UNC Press, 1926), 28f.
[102] C. Vann Woodward noted that in the Southern states east of the Mississippi, 96.6 percent of church members were Protestant. In North Carolina, however, the percentage stood higher at 99.4 percent. The oldest church in Carteret County is St. Paul's Episcopal Church in Beaufort. Established as an Anglican church, Bell Chapel, in 1723, its affiliation was changed to Episcopal in 1855. The county also has a large Roman Catholic Church, St. Egbert, in Morehead City. Established in the late 1920s, St. Egbert was named for a Passionist priest, Father Egbert Albert. Father Egbert preached to Carteret County residents from a railway car. Legend has it that, threatened by a mob after "preaching to dispel anti-Catholic ignorance," Father Egbert "warned the people of God's displeasure if his messages were not well received, and left . . . directly thereafter a major fire struck the town [Morehead City], and a committee was sent to ask Father Egbert to return. Woodward, *Origins of New South*, 449; "A Brief History of St. Paul's Church Beaufort, North Carolina"; "The Legend of Father Egbert Albert."
[103] Gerry Campbell, "History of Atlantic Beach," Davis and Hamilton, eds., *Heritage of Carteret County*, 160.
[104] Ibid., 162.
[105] Ibid., 160.
[106] Hoffman to Judge, Hoffman Papers.
[107] Alice Hoffman to Francis E. Curtis, 19 June 1921 and 23 June 1921; Alice Hoffman to John Judge, 19 June 192l; Alice Hoffman to Bush, 3 July 1921, Hoffman Papers.
[108] United States Post Office Department Reports of Site Locations 1837-1950 and *Record of Appointment of Postmaster 1832-September 30, 1971, Record Group 28*,

National Archives (Washington, DC), quoted in Charles O. Pitts, unpublished manuscript.
[109] Furnifold M. Simmons to General A.S. Burleson, 26 May 1920, quoted in Pitts.
[110] Alice Hoffman to _____, 6 July 1921, Hoffman Papers.
[111] Alice Hoffman to Maggie Duplanty, 21 January 1924, Hoffman Papers.
[112] Alice Hoffman to _____, 24 January 1924, Hoffman Papers.
[113] United States Post Office Department, First Assistant Postmaster General (Washington, DC, 5 January 1924).
[114] Hoffman was partially correct. On July 12, 1813, months before the British sailed up Chesapeake Bay and destroyed portions of Washington, DC, "a British fleet of one large battleship and over one hundred smaller craft, including barges, all under the command of Admiral Cockburn, landed at Ocracoke and Portsmouth, but not considering North Carolina a major objective, the fleet sailed away four days later." "War of 1812," Hill, ed., *Historic Carteret*, 50.
[115] Alice Hoffman to Herbert Weinstock, 28 February 1944, Hoffman Papers.
[116] Alice Hoffman to Eleanor Roosevelt, 9 January 1943, Hoffman Papers.
[117] Alice Hoffman to Arthur H. Haaren, 6 August 1929, Hoffman Papers.
[118] Phillips, "Woman of Mystery," Pitts, ed., *Heritage of Carteret County*, 382.
A consistent and long-held story among Salter Path people is of a German, a Mr. Ferringhaus, renting a small home in Salter Path from George and Juanita Smith about two years before WWII broke out. He was a pleasant, blond-haired man in his 30s who spoke perfect English. He spent his time measuring and mapping the beach and left suddenly and mysteriously right after the war began. Hoffman is often linked with him in the villagers' memories. Although an intriguing side note, it is not the focus of this work and I have no further information about this man.
[119] As well as the rumors in World War II, after World War I, in a letter to Hoffman's attorneys, Satterlee and Canfield, John Royall wrote on 6 April 1925: "I have been beset by all manner of annoyances arising out of the sale of this property to Mrs. Hoffman, even including several investigations by the Department of Justice who investigated her during the war, which I denounced at the time as a damnable outrage. In consequence, my own loyalty was questioned for having sold her the property." Ibid., 385.
[120] Frank M. Wooten to Federal Bureau of Investigation, 11 April 1942, Wooten Papers.
[121] Edward Scheidt, Special Agent in Charge, to Frank M. Wooten, 20 April 1942, Hoffman Papers.
[122] Alice Hoffman to _____, Hoffman Papers.
[123] "Salter Path," Hill, ed., *Historic Carteret*, 100.
[124] Analysis of Title, Frank M. Wooten Papers, unedited collection, East Carolina Manuscript Collection, J.Y. Joyner Library, East Carolina University, Greenville, NC.
[125] David S. Cecelski, "The Hidden World of Mullet Camps: AfricanAmerican Architecture on the North Carolina Coast," *The North Carolina Historical Review* Vol. 70 (January 1993), 1.
[126] Ibid., 3.

[127] Robert Sullivan, "Modern Life Set to Invade Salter Path," *New York Sunday News*, 7 October 1945, 56f.
[128] Index to births 1913-1957 Carteret County, Carteret County Register of Deeds Office, Beaufort, NC, 54, 172-E, 62.
[129] Marriage Register-Carteret County, North Carolina, Carteret County Register of Deeds Office, Beaufort, NC, 117-V, 117-Y, 57-J.
[130] Joel G. Hancock, *Strengthened by the Storm* (Morehead City: Campbell & Campbell, Publishers, 1988), 12.
[131] David Stick, *The Outer Banks of North Carolina 1584-1958* (Chapel Hill, 1958), 193.
[132] Ben Dixon MacNeill, "North Carolina Village Has Practiced Real Socialism for Over Two Centuries and Is Model of Civic Virtue," *News and Observer*, 2 May 1926, Editorial Section, 1ff.
[133] *Beaufort News*, 16 April 1918, Volume IX, No. 37.
[134] McCajah Adams to Alice Hoffman, 18 February 1918, Hoffman Papers.
[135] John A. Royall to Herbert Satterlee and George F. Canfield, 23 October 1924, Hoffman Papers.
[136] Alice Hoffman to Sam Duplanty, 30 August 1920, Hoffman Papers.
[137] Although Hoffman's attorney, Frank Wooten Jr., referred often to the suit brought against Hoffman by David John Willis, the author has not been able to find any record of the suit. It may have never come before the court, been dismissed and not recorded, or lost.
[138] Alice Hoffman to Sam Duplanty, 11 April 1920, Hoffman Papers.
[139] Alice Hoffman to James Connell, I5 February 1926, Hoffman Papers.
[140] Alice Hoffman to Julius Duncan, 17 May 1919, Hoffman Papers.
[141] Ibid. As to the legality of livestock owned by Salter Path residents grazing on Hoffman's property, historian Edward Ayers noted that "for as long as people could remember, much of the South had been open range. Families who owned cows or pigs simply marked them, allowed them to fend for themselves, and then rounded them up when it came time for slaughter. The new laws, [in the late 1800s] which required owners to fence their livestock, made it virtually impossible for the landless to keep animals. Political battles raged for decades over these laws." This controversy also raged in Carteret County for many years between the bankers and Hoffman. Edward Ayers, *The Promise of the New South Life After Reconstruction* (New York: Oxford University Press, 1992), 189.

Chapter Three

[142] Alice Hoffman to Francis E. Curtis, 23 October 1933, Hoffman Papers.
[143] Alice Hoffman to _____ Norris, 28 January 1930, Hoffman Papers.
[144] Ibid.
[145] David Stick, *Graveyard of the Atlantic* (Chapel Hill, NC: 1952), viii; Ibid., 144.
[146] Alice Hoffman to Karl T. Frederick, 17 July 1923, Hoffman Papers.
[147] Alice Hoffman to Julius Duncan, 26 July 191, Hoffman Papers.
[148] H.C. Yarrow, quoted in Stick, *Graveyard*, 213f.

[149] Alice Hoffman to Herbert Satterlee, 23 April 1920, Hoffman Papers.
[150] Stick, *Outer Banks*, 232.
[151] Profits were divided into shares, with each man receiving one share. For dories, nets, and other equipment, each received a share which contributed to their maintenance.
[152] Julius Duncan to Alice Hoffman, 25 August 1919; Alice Hoffman to Julius Duncan, 26 July 1919, Hoffman Papers.
[153] Alice Hoffman to Sam Duplanty, 22 April 1920, Hoffman Papers.
[154] Ruth Barbour, "Views on Mrs. Hoffman vary," *Carteret County News-Times*, 31 May 1991, 12A.
[155] Alice Hoffman to Francis E. Curtis, 11 October 1923, Hoffman Papers.
[156] Carteret County, NC, Agreement, Wooten Papers.
[157] Ibid.
[158] Sam Duplanty to Alice Hoffman, 27 July 1924, Hoffman Papers.
[159] Alice Hoffman to Francis E. Curtis, 23 October 1933, Hoffman Papers. Hoffman later calculated her investment in the plant at $54,555. Money Advanced . . . For Fish Fertilizer Industry, 23 March 1939, Wooten Papers.
[160] "Good Old Days," *Carteret County News-Times*, 30 September 1958, 10A.
[161] Alice Hoffman to James Connell. 15 February 1926, Hoffman Papers.
[162] Alice Hoffman to Herbert Satterlee and George F. Canfield, 24 December 1929, Hoffman Papers. Phillip's fish factory burned in 1953, the year of Hoffman's death. The estimated loss was more than $100,000. Charles O. Pitts, "As We Were," *Carteret County News-Times*, 6 October 1993, 16A.
[163] Hoffman autobiography.
[164] Alice Hoffman to Lester D. Egbert, 25 February 1931, Hoffman Papers.
[165] Lefferts, Lay, and Lewis, *UNC Extension Bulletin*, 75f. Lefferts attributed the failure of Carteret County farmers to supply food to four causes: "1. Lack of ready cash markets; 2. Lack of cooperation among county farmers; 3. The excessive growing of tobacco and cotton; 4. Lack of modern methods of cultivation and management."
[166] Alice Hoffman to Sam Duplanty, 18 June 1920, Hoffman Papers.
[167] Alice Hoffman to Department of Agriculture, Raleigh, NC, 2 April 1919, Hoffman Papers.
[168] William Moore to Alice Hoffman, 22 July 1919, Hoffman Papers.
[169] Moore to Hoffman, September, 19, 1919, Hoffman Papers.
[170] David A. Lockmiller, *History of the North Carolina State College of Agriculture and Engineering of the University of North Carolina 1889-1939* (Raleigh, NC: Edwards & Broughton Company, 1939), 23, 105. William S. Powell, *North Carolina through Four Centuries* (Chapel Hill, NC: University of North Carolina Press, 1989), 467.
[171] Ruth Barbour, "Dairy days on Bogue Banks," *Carteret County News-Times*, 17 March 1991, 8A.
[172] Ibid.
[173] Alice Hoffman to Sam Duplanty, 5 June 1920, Hoffman Papers.
[174] Ibid.
[175] Alice Hoffman to John Judge, 28 August 1923, Hoffman Papers.

[176] Lester D. Egbert to Alice Hoffman, 20 January 1926, Hoffman Papers.
[177] Ibid.
[178] C.T. Gillikin to Alice Hoffman, 21 May 1925, Hoffman Papers.
[179] Alice Hoffman to F.F. Field, 31 March 1919, Hoffman Papers.
[180] Alice Hoffman to Sam Duplanty, 17 June 1919, Hoffman Papers.
[181] Alice Hoffman to Francis E. Curtis, 6 June 1921, Hoffman Papers.
[182] Hoffman autobiography. Tick bites can cause Anaplasmosis, an infectious disease of cattle, sheep, and goats, common to the southeastern United States. Anaplasmosis Information for the Cattle Industry of North Carolina, North Carolina Department of Agriculture, 1994.
[183] James Connell to Alice Hoffman, 31 October 1925, Hoffman Papers.
[184] Alice Hoffman to John Royall, 10 August 1920, Wooten Papers.
[185] Ibid.
[186] Ibid.
[187] Clerk of Court Office, Carteret County Courthouse, Beaufort, NC, Minute Docket 8, p. 114, cases 35 and 36, Judge M.V. Barnhill, presiding.
[188] Alice Hoffman to John A. Royall, 3 September 1920, Wooten Papers.
[189] Ibid.
[190] Alice Hoffman to Francis E. Curtis, 9 July 1923, Hoffman Papers.
[191] James Connell to Alice Hoffman, 4 November 1925, Hoffman Papers.
[192] James Connell to Alice Hoffman, 9 February 1926, Hoffman Papers.
[193] Alice Hoffman to James Connell, 15 February 1926, Hoffman Papers.
[194] Alice Hoffman to ____Brookbank, 28 November 1920, Hoffman Papers. A highly infectious disease, tuberculosis can be transmitted from cattle to humans through their milk.
[195] Arthur Jenkins to Alice Hoffman, 12 July 1921, Hoffman Papers.
[196] Alice Hoffman to Francis E. Curtis, 11 August 1921; Alice Hoffman to _Cox, 22 February 1922, Hoffman Papers.
[197] Alice Hoffman to Francis E. Curtis, 11 August 1921, Hoffman Papers.
[198] Alice Hoffman to Sam Duplanty, 17 July 1924, Hoffman Papers.
[199] Maggie Duplanty to Alice Hoffman, 10 July 1924, Hoffman Papers.
[200] Ibid.
[201] Alice Hoffman to Francis E. Curtis, 24 May 1927, Hoffman Papers. Duplanty bought a farm of his own on the mainland just west of Morehead City. He had been in and out of the hospital with stomach problems for many years. The Duplantys, if they did separate, must have reunited. Duplantys's daughter never mentioned a separation and stated, “After my father died following a gall bladder operation, my mother and I soon moved back to New York. That might have been about 1930.” Barbour, “Views on Mrs. Hoffman vary.”
[202] Marshallburg is located in the “Down East” section of Carteret County, on the mainland east of Beaufort.
[203] Monroe Lewis to Alice Hoffman, 5 April 1928, Hoffman Papers.
[204] Alice Hoffman to Francis E. Curtis, 5 May 1929, Hoffman Papers.
[205] John H. Judge to Alice Hoffman, 29 July 1927, Hoffman Papers.

[206] Maggie Duplanty to E.H. Gorham, 4 July 1927, Hoffman Papers.
[207] Ibid.
[208] Alice Hoffman to M.M, 30 August 1927, Hoffman Papers.
[209] Clerk of Court Office, Carteret County Courthouse, Beaufort, NC, Minute docket 8, 19 October 1928, R.A. Nunn, judge presiding.
[210] The association's headquarters are located in Brattleboro, Vermont.
[211] Alice Hoffman to Arthur H. Haaren, 6 August 1929, Hoffman Papers.
[212] E. Abbott to Alice Hoffman, 21 November 1929, Hoffman Papers.
[213] Clerk of Court Office, Carteret County Courthouse, Beaufort, NC, Minute docket 10, p. 44, case 40, June 1926, Marshall T. Spears, judge presiding.
[214] Alice Hoffman to Maurice Strum, 14 April 1938, Hoffman Papers.

Chapter Four

[215] Robert W. Semenow, *Questions And Answers on Real Estate* (Englewood Cliffs, NJ, 1969), 177.
[216] Hoffman autobiography.
[217] Julius Duncan to Alice Hoffman, 25 August 1919, Hoffman Papers.
[218] Alice Hoffman to John Judge, 28 August 1923, Hoffman Papers.
[219] Alice Hoffman to Francis E. Curtis, 24 June 1923, Hoffman Papers.
[220] Ibid.
[221] North Carolina Superior Court, Carteret County, Beaufort, NC, Judgment, Alice Hoffman v. J. C. Lewis, et al., June Term, 1923.
[222] Alice Hoffman to Francis E. Curtis, 24 June 1923, Hoffman Papers.
[223] Alice Hoffman to Henry K. Fort, 9 July 1923, Hoffman Papers.
[224] NC Superior Court, June Term, 1923. Claude Wheatly III, grandson of Claude Wheatly, said that according to his grandfather, the court was determined that Hoffman should not be allowed to evict the villagers. Personal interview by author, 16 July 1993.
[225] Alice Hoffman to Francis E. Curtis, 24 June 1923, Hoffman Papers.
[226] In another letter, Hoffman wrote that the costs arising from the suit amounted to $1125. This probably included surveys of the Salter Path property. Alice Hoffman to Karl T. Frederick, 17 July 1923, Hoffman Papers.
[227] Hoffman wrote: "When Mr. Royall & I signed the contract he requested me to take in exchange for a tract of land he had originally included in the area for which a price was agreed upon, the area involved in this servitude. This was because the title to the original piece was not clear, in fact he did not have it, for I bought it through another source later. He volunteered to try to get title to it, & gave me an option for which I was to pay $6750." Alice Hoffman to John Judge, 28 August 1923, Hoffman Papers.
[228] Ibid.
[229] Alice Hoffman to Herbert Satterlee and George F. Canfield, 24 December 1929, Hoffman Papers.
[230] Herbert Satterlee, for Satterlee and Canfield, to Alice Hoffman, 13 December 1929, Hoffman Papers.
[231] Ibid.

[232] Herbert Satterlee to Alice Hoffman, 22 November 1928, Hoffman Papers.
[233] Alice Hoffman v. John A. Royall, North Carolina Superior Court, Carteret County Courthouse, Beaufort, NC, Minute book 10, p 44, case 28, F.A. Daniels, presiding judge.
[234] Henry K. Fort to Alice Hoffman, 4 July 1923, Hoffman Papers.
[235] Alice Hoffman to Francis E. Curtis, 24 May 1927, Hoffman Papers.
[236] Alice Hoffman to Francis E. Curtis, 15 July 1923, Hoffman Papers.
[237] State of North Carolina, County of Carteret, Carteret County Courthouse, Beaufort, NC, Henry K. Fort, Petitioner v. Mrs. A. Hoffman, et al., Report of Examiner, No. 509 S.P.D., 15 October 1925.
[238] Fort v. Hoffman, 15 October 1925.
[239] Ibid.
[240] State of North Carolina, Carteret County, Carteret County Courthouse, Beaufort, NC, Henry K. Fort v. Mrs. Alice Hoffman, et al, Exception to Examiner's Report, 15 December 1925.
[241] Carteret County Register of Deeds Office, Beaufort, NC, North Carolina Book W, 253.
[242] Ibid.; Henry K. Fort v. J.C. Lewis, Arthur Smith, and Dexter Smith, Writ of Possession, 17 April 1926.
[243] John A. Royall to Satterlee and Canfield, 23 October 1924, Hoffman Papers.
[244] George Flint Warren Jr. to Alice Hoffman, 10 July 1928, Hoffman Papers.
[245] Alice Hoffman to Lester D. Egbert, 19 February 1933, Hoffman Papers.
[246] Alice Hoffman to Francis E. Curtis, 23 October 1933, Hoffman Papers.
[247] Ibid.
[248] Hoffman to Curtis, Hoffman Papers.
[249] Ibid. Contrastingly, Hoffman wrote a few months later that "Mr. Phillips looks ten years older, which naturally distresses his family & for which I get all the credit!!!" Rumor has it that Hoffman fell in love with Phillips. Alice Hoffman to Lester D. Egbert, 1 January 1934, Hoffman Papers.
[250] Points of Difference Between Mrs. Hoffman & Llewellyn Phillips, 15 May 1939, Wooten Papers.
[251] Alice Hoffman to Lester D. Egbert, 15 May 1929. Hoffman Papers.
[252] Alice Hoffman to Raymond Harper, 27 October 1938, Hoffman Papers.
[253] Carteret County Office of Deeds, Book 74, page 563, Carteret County Registry, Beaufort, North Carolina.
[254] Alice Hoffman to Raymond Harper, 28 July 1938, Hoffman Papers.
[255] Judgments against Mrs. Alice Hoffman, 2 January 1948, Wooten Papers. Among them were Satterlee and Canfield for $29,224.67; Atlas Storage Company for $12,511.52; Edward Blum for $5,282.03; Louis Friedman for $26,409.41; Charles Jacobsen for $1,296.48; Union Indemnity Company for $1,950.35; Daisy Judge [widow of Hoffman's first attorney, John H. Judge] for an unspecified amount. These debts total $74,724.11, without the Judge debt. Amazingly, in 1943, Hoffman wrote her accountant, Maurice Strum, that he was "misinformed about the Atlas [Storage Company]. I never

had any dealings with them." Alice Hoffman to Maurice Strum, 15 February 1943, Hoffman Papers.

[256] Summons, Louis H. Pink v. Mrs. Alice Hoffman, 6 August 1926, Wooten Papers.

[257] Ibid.

[258] Alice Hoffman to Bernice _____, 4 July 1941, Hoffman Papers.

[259] Points of Difference, Wooten Papers.

[260] Alice Hoffman to S.S. Szlapka, 14 May 1939, Hoffman Papers.

[261] Ibid.

[262] Points of Difference, Wooten Papers,

[263] Alice Hoffman to S.S. Szlapka letter, 14 May 1939, Hoffman Papers.

[264] Hoffman autobiography.

[265] John Marshall Matthias, born in Van Wert, Ohio, graduated Ohio State University in Columbus, passed the bar on 11 February 1931, served two terms in the Ohio Legislature, acted as Columbus municipal judge, and served, as his father before him, as Ohio Supreme Court Justice from 1954-1971. Matthias died 25 January 1973. *Who Was Who in America Volume V* (Chicago: Marquis Who's Who, Inc., 1973), 466. According to recollections of Matthias's son, John Matthias, his parents had recently married and they thought the trip to North Carolina might be something of a honeymoon. Arriving on Bogue Banks, they met Hoffman, a strange elderly woman living in a bizarre house. The doors and windows remained closed and locked, allowing no air to circulate. Candles offered the only light, and they listened to stories of frightful and disgusting natives. John E. Matthias, interview by author, telephone, 19 April 1994.

[266] Alice Hoffman to S.S. Szlapka, 26 June 1939, Hoffman Papers.

[267] Ibid.

[268] Alice Hoffman to Maurice Strum, 24 March 1939, Hoffman Papers.

[269] Alice Hoffman to S.S. Szlapka, 26 June 1939, Hoffman Papers. Hoffman was then seventy-seven years old.

[270] Alice Jacoby recalled that Hoffman bought Matthias a car for his troubles and a diamond ring for his wife, Lois. Alice Jacoby, interview by author, telephone, 19 April 1994. After the court's decision, Hoffman wrote Ehringhaus and accused him of allowing his name to become associated with a questionable legal action. Ehringhaus replied: "I counseled you to secure your own legal advice, and rejoiced when your kinsman . . . came to look out for your interests . . . I have been frank and aboveboard with him . . . You and he had also the benefit of the wise counsel of his very able and learned father, Judge Matthias . . . This is written to put the record straight . . . I sincerely regret that you are troubled . . . bear in mind that Mr. Matthias is making a real effort to bring about a situation which I am sure will please you . . . he deserves your . . . confidence." J.C.B. Ehringhaus to Alice Hoffman, August 7, 1939, Wooten Papers. Hoffman penned at the bottom of the letter: "This was and is not so."

[271] Frank Wooten Jr. to Leslie Davis, 30 April 1940, Wooten Papers.

[272] Alice Hoffman to Mary Matthias, 20 January 1941, Wooten Papers.

[273] Alice Hoffman to Mary Matthias, 29 December 1941, Wooten Papers.

[274] Ibid.

[275] Frank Wooten Jr. to Eleanor Roosevelt, 28 April 1942, Wooten Papers.

[276] Analysis of Title, Section III, Chapter 3, Wooten Papers.
[277] Aycock Brown, "Thrice-A-Week Mail," *News and Observer*, Raleigh, NC, 8 September 1940, 4M.
[278] Ibid.
[279] Alice Hoffman to E.V. Webb, 15 June 1940, Hoffman Papers.
[280] Frank M. Wooten Jr. to Alice Hoffman, 20 May 1940, Wooten Papers.
[281] Eleanor Roosevelt to Alice Hoffman, 1940, Hoffman Papers.
[282] Roosevelt to Hoffman, Wooten Papers. Roosevelt must have been referring to the fact that the property had been foreclosed upon and sold at auction by the county for nonpayment of taxes.
[283] Hoffman autobiography.
[284] Eleanor Roosevelt to Alice Hoffman, 1940, Hoffman Papers.
[285] Carteret County, North Carolina, quit-claim deed, Wooten Papers.
[286] Alice Hoffman to Eleanor Roosevelt, 28 July 1940, Hoffman Papers.
[287] Hoffman Papers. Apparently, Matthias was attempting to settle the Crump lien by the sale of a portion of the property. Also, seemingly, the road problem had not been solved to Hoffman's satisfaction. Hoffman, in this same letter wrote, "Miss Kaye, whom I have known in Washington for some time has come down to help me with my writing this summer, & she was compelled to sit in this heat, on my private road, while a truck of watermelons which was stuck in the sand was unloaded. Imagine how exasperating if one were on the way to catch a train!!!"
[288] North Carolina, Carteret County indenture, Wooten Papers.
[289] Frank Wooten Jr. to Alice Hoffman, 27 August 1940. Hoffman Papers.
[290] Ibid.
[291] Carteret County Superior Court, Special August Civil Term, Final Judgment, 1944, Henry L. Stevens, judge presiding, Wooten Papers.
[292] Ibid.
[293] Ibid.
[294] Order of the Clerk of the Superior Court of Carteret County, confirmed by J. Paul Frizzelle, Resident Judge of the Fifth Judicial District of the Superior Court of North Carolina, Carteret County Courthouse, Beaufort, North Carolina.

Chapter Five

[295] "Mrs. Alice G. Hoffman Died Sunday after Long Illness," *Carteret County News-Times*, 17 March 1953, Front Page.
[296] Alexandra Roosevelt Dworkin, interview by author, telephone, 7 February 1994.
[297] Ibid.
[298] Alice Jacoby, interview by author, telephone, 19 April 1994.
[299] Ibid.
[300] Hoffman to Kingsley, 1929, Hoffman Papers.
[301] Ibid.
[302] Ibid.
[303] Bernice _____ to Alice Hoffman, 3 June 1940, Hoffman Papers.

[304] Hoffman to Duplanty, November 19, 1922, Hoffman Papers.
[305] Alice Hoffman to Mary Matthias, 20 January 1941, Hoffman Papers.
[306] Herbert Weinstock to Alice Hoffman, 14 February 1944, Hoffman Papers.
[307] Alice Hoffman to Alfred A. Knopf, 9 February 1944, Hoffman Papers.
[308] Alice Hoffman to William Kingsley, 9 November 1929, Hoffman Papers; Alice Hoffman to Frank Wooten, Hoffman Papers.
[309] Joel Hancock, interview by author, telephone, 22 March 1994.

Conclusion

[310] MacNeill, "North Carolina Village Has Practiced Real Socialism."
[311] Ben Hogwood, "Tax breaks no cure for ailing commercial fishing industry," *The Carteret County News-Times*, March 28, 2010.
[312] Barbara Allen quoted in *Sense of Place: American Regional Cultures* (Lexington, Kentucky: The University Press of Kentucky, 1990), 1.

SELECTED BIBLIOGRAPHY

Manuscripts

Alice Green Hoffman autobiography. Alice Green Hoffman Papers, Collection No. 127.49, East. Carolina Manuscript Room, J.Y. Joyner Library, East Carolina University, Greenville, NC. 131.

Partial autobiography, arranged topically, reminiscences of Hoffman's childhood, travels, and financial difficulties.

Alice Green Hoffman Papers, Collection No. 127, East Carolina Manuscript Room, J.Y. Joyner Library, East Carolina University, Greenville, NC.

Large collection which includes correspondence, financial and legal papers, farm records, and miscellaneous items.

Frank M. Wooten Jr. Papers. Unedited Collection, East Carolina Manuscript Room, J.Y. Joyner Library, East Carolina University, Greenville, NC.

Collection donated by Hoffman's last attorney, Frank M. Wooten, Jr., including correspondence, legal papers, deeds, and court records.

Pitts, Charles O. Unpublished manuscript of exhaustive research project concerning the histories of all Carteret County post offices.

General Histories and Monographs

Ayers, Edward L. *The Promise of the New South Life After Reconstruction.* New York: Oxford University Press, 1992.

History on the development of the New South which emphasizes social and cultural changes which occurred in the latter half of the nineteenth century.

Bertelson, David. *The Lazy South*. New York: Oxford University Press, 1967.

Excellent historical analysis of the causes for the erroneous supposition that laziness is a Southern attribute.

Butler, Lindley S, and Alan D. Watson. *The North Carolina Experience*. Chapel Hill, NC: The University of North Carolina Press, 1984.

Collection of papers, speeches, documents, newspaper articles throughout North Carolina history. Helpful bibliographies at conclusion of each chapter.

Connor, R.D.W. *North Carolina Rebuilding an Ancient Commonwealth* 1584-1925. Chicago: The American Historical Society, Inc., 1929.

Collection of short biographies of notable North Carolinians which contains a contemporary description of J.C.B. Ehringhaus.

Davis, Pat Dula and Kathleen Hill Hamilton, eds. *The Heritage of Carteret County, North Carolina, Vol. I*. Winston-Salem, NC: Hunter Publishing Company, 1982.

Collection of memoirs, articles, and short histories concerning Carteret County. The author used the following articles:

Alford, Michael B. "A Look at the Historical Watercraft of Carteret County."

Branch, Paul. "World War II and Carteret County."

Campbell, Gerry. "History of Atlantic Beach."

Paul, Daphne. "The Sea Breeze Theatre (1910-30)."

Phillips, Ethel C. "'Woman of Mystery'-Alice Grene [*sic*] Hoffman."

Reintjes, John W. and Marcus J. Hepburn. "Historical Role of Fishing in Carteret County."

Tugman, Cindy. "Life in Morehead City."

Escott, Paul D. and David R. Goldfield. *Major Problems in the History of the American South Volume II: The New South.* Lexington, MA: D.C. Heath and Company, 1990.

Collection of essays by numerous historians with differing opinions and assessments of events in the South.

Fite, Gilbert C. *Cotton Fields No More Southern Agriculture 1865-1980.* Lexington, KY: The University Press of Kentucky, 1984.

General history of the development of modern farming methods in the South.

Gowan, Robert J. *Of Tar Heel Towns, Shipbuilders, Reconstructionists and Alliancemen Papers in North Carolina History.* Greenville, NC: East Carolina University Publications, 1981.

Collection of four essays which analyze subjects in North Carolina history neglected by historians.

Hancock, Joel. *Strengthened by the Storm.* Morehead City, NC: Campbell & Campbell Publishers, 1988.

An account by a local historian of the establishment of the Mormon Church on Harkers Island, North Carolina.

Hill, Mrs. Fred, ed. *Historical Carteret County North Carolina, 1663-1975.*

A collection of short articles concerning local affairs, places, and events. The author used "War of 1812" and "Salter Path."

Link, William A. and Arthur S. Link. *American Epoch A History of the United States since 1900 Volume I: War, Reform, and Society 1900-1945.* New York: McGraw-Hill, Inc., 1993.

An excellent account of American history in the Twentieth Century.

Mayer, Grace M. *Once upon a City.* New York: The Macmillan Company, 1958.

History, largely pictorial, of New York City from the exclusive Manhattan residences to the slum areas.

A Pictorial Review of Morehead City History Through 1981. Greenville, NC: Highland Press of Greenville, 1982.

A collection of articles concerning the establishment and development of Morehead City and Atlantic Beach. The author used "Railroad" and "Atlantic Beach."

Pilkey, Orrin and J. Andrew G. Cooper. *The Last Beach*. Durham, NC: Duke University Press, 2014.

Pilkey, Orrin, Jr., Orrin Pilkey, Sr., and Robb Turner. *How to Live with an Island: A Handbook to Bogue Banks, North Carolina*. Raleigh, NC: North Carolina Department of Natural and Economic Resources, 1975.

Conservationist account of the destructive and careless development of Bogue Banks with suggestions on better property management.

Powell, William S. *North Carolina Through Four Centuries*. Chapel Hill, NC: The University of North Carolina Press, 1989.

A non-interpretive history of North Carolina. Not very useful.

Semenow, Robert W. *Questions And Answers on Real Estate*. Englewood Cliffs, NJ: Prentice-Hall, Inc., 1969.

Definitions of real estate and property concepts and terms.

Stick, David. *Graveyard of the Atlantic Shipwrecks off the North Carolina* Coast. Chapel Hill, NC: The University of North Carolina Press, 1952.

Intriguing historical account of shipwrecks through three centuries and development of the Life-Saving Service, forerunner of the United States Coast Guard.

—— *The Outer Banks of North Carolina 1584-1958*. Chapel Hill, NC: The University of North Carolina Press, 1958.

A fine history of the barrier islands and small communities of the North Carolina coast.

Stover, John F. *The Railroads of the South 1865-1900 A Study in Finance and Control.* Chapel Hill, NC: The University of North Carolina Press, 1955.

Historical study of the development of the railroad system in the South, both antebellum and postbellum.

Van Loon, Dirk. *The Family Cow.* Charlotte, Vermont: Garden Way Publishing, 1976.

An informative book on the care of dairy cows on small farms including a short history of cattle breeds.

Wharton, Edith. *Roman Fever and Other Stories.* New York: Berkley Books, 1981.

Fictional stories of New York City upper class at the turn of the century. The author used the introduction by Marilyn French.

Woodward, C. Vann. *Origins of the New South 1877-1913.* Baton Rouge, Louisiana: Louisiana State University Press, 1971.

A seminal work on development in the South after Reconstruction.

Wrenn, Tony. *Beaufort North Carolina.* Falls Church, VA: EconoPrint, 1970.

A short history of Beaufort, North Carolina, with an emphasis on its historical homes.

Newspapers

Beaufort News. Beaufort, North Carolina.

The Carteret County News-Times. Morehead City, NC.

The News and Observer. Raleigh, North Carolina.

Sunday Times. New York City, New York.

Periodicals

Cecelski, David S. "The Hidden World of Mullet Camps: African American Architecture on the North Carolina Coast." *The North Carolina Historical Review* Vol. 70 No. 1. January 1993.

Government Documents

Clerk of Court, Minute Docket, Carteret County Courthouse, Beaufort, North Carolina.

Index to Births, Register of Deeds Office, Carteret County Courthouse, Beaufort, North Carolina.

Marriage Register, Register of Deeds Office, Carteret County Courthouse, Beaufort, North Carolina.

North Carolina Superior Court Documents, Beaufort, North Carolina.
Alice Hoffman v. J.C. Lewis, et al.
Alice Hoffman v. David John Willis.
Alice Hoffman v. Henry Willis and David John Willis.
Alice Hoffman v. John A. Royall.
Alice Hoffman v. J.M. Willis, S.A. Duplanty, and C.S. Wallace.
Alice Hoffman v. E. Abbott.
Alice Hoffman v. John Marshall Matthias and Roosevelt children.
Alice Hoffman v. Llewellyn Phillips.
Alice Hoffman, Bogue Banks, Inc. v. Llewellyn Phillips, John Marshall Matthias, The Alden Corporation and R.N. Lorrimer, 1943.
Alice Hoffman, Bogue Banks, Inc. v. Llewellyn Phillips, John Marshall Matthias, The Alden Corporation and R.N. Lorrimer, 1944.
Henry K. Fort v. J.C. Lewis, et al. Report of Examiner.
Henry K. Fort v. Alice Hoffman. Exception to Examiner's Report.
Henry K. Fort v. J.C. Lewis, et al. Writ of Possession.
County of Carteret v. J.L. Austin, et al.

Record of Appointments of Postmasters 1832-September 30, 1971, Record Group 28. The National Archives, Washington, DC.

United States Post Office Reports of Site Locations 1837-1950. The National Archives, Washington, DC.

Personal Interviews

Dworkin, Alexandra Roosevelt. 9 February 1994.

Hancock, Joel. 22 March 1994.

Jacoby, Alice. 19 April 1994.

Matthias, John E. 19 April 1994.

McNamara. J. Paul. 19 April 1994.

Norman, Adrienne. 2 April 1993.

Wheatly, III, Claude. 16 July 1993.

Miscellaneous Sources

Anaplasmosis Information for the Cattle Industry of North Carolina.

Pamphlet from College of Agriculture and Life Sciences, North Carolina State University, Raleigh, NC.

Automated Archives, Inc. Screen 4996. 1993. The State Library of Ohio, Columbus, Ohio.

Computer information service of the library which included information concerning John Marshall Matthias.

Bell, H. Mack, II. Historiographer for the Episcopal Diocese of East Carolina, Kinston, North Carolina.

Information concerning the gift of property to the Episcopal diocese from the Roosevelt heirs.

"History of St. Egbert Albert."

Pamphlet from St. Egbert Roman Catholic Church, Morehead City, NC.

"The History of St. Paul's Episcopal Church Beaufort North Carolina."

Pamphlet from St. Paul's Episcopal Church, Beaufort. NC.

Matthias, John E. "Poem in Three Parts Part Three." Bucyrus. Swallow Press, 1970.

National Cyclopaedia of American Biography. New York: J.T. White & Company, 1962.

Probate information for John Marshall Matthias. Ohio State Superior Court Law Library. Columbus, Ohio.

Seale, Dorothy Weiser. *Matthias Milestones*. Columbus, Ohio, 1984.

Who Was Who in America Volume V 1969-1973. Chicago: Marquis Who's Who, Inc., 1973.

APPENDIX A

Original Thesis Documents

Kathleen McMillan Guthrie. ALICE GREEN HOFFMAN: QUEEN OF BOGUE BANKS. (Under the direction of Dr. Henry Ferrell) Department of History, May 1994.

The purpose of this thesis is the examination and assessment of the life of Alice Green Hoffman. Hoffman's papers, located in Joyner Library, East Carolina University, are the primary source of material for this thesis. Frank M. Wooten, Jr., Hoffman's last attorney, also donated his papers to Joyner Library. Wooten's papers include his correspondence with Hoffman and legal documents concerning Hoffman's litigation. This collection added considerably to the interpretation.

ALICE GREEN HOFFMAN:
QUEEN OF BOGUE BANKS

A Thesis

Presented to

the Faculty of the Department of History

East Carolina University

In Partial Fulfillment

of the Requirements for the Degree

Master of Arts in History

by

Kathleen McMillan Guthrie

May 1994

ALICE GREEN HOFFMAN: QUEEN OF BOGUE BANKS

by

Kathleen McMillan Guthrie

APPROVED BY:

DIRECTOR OF THESIS ______________________
Dr. Henry C. Ferrell

COMMITTEE MEMBER ______________________
Dr. Fred D. Ragan

COMMITTEE MEMBER ______________________
Dr. Donald H. Parkerson

COMMITTEE MEMBER ______________________
Dr. Susan M. McCammon

CHAIR OF THE DEPARTMENT OF HISTORY ______________________
Dr. Mary Jo Bratton

INTERIM DEAN OF THE GRADUATE SCHOOL ______________________
Dr. Therese G. Lawler

APPENDIX B

Partial Chronology of Events

1862	Alice Green [Hoffman] born in New York City, New York.
1870	Hoffman's mother, Mary Frances Crouch Green, dies.
1882?	Hoffman's grandfather, Theron Butler, dies.
Early 1880s	Hoffman's father, Albert Green, dies.
Late 1880s	Hoffman makes several trips to Europe.
Early 1890s	Hoffman rents cottage in Southampton, Massachusetts.
1892	Hoffman rents house in Paris, France.
1895	Hoffman moves to Paris.
1909 or 1910	Hoffman marries John Ellis Hoffman in Paris.
1910	Hoffman returns to New York City.
1910 or 1911	Hoffman divorces John Ellis Hoffman.
1912	Hoffman's niece, Eleanor Roosevelt, returns to New York City from San Francisco, California.
1915	Hoffman visits Bogue Banks, North Carolina.
1917	Hoffman purchases Bogue Banks property from John A. Royall.
1917	Hoffman establishes Pine Grove Farms on Bogue Banks.
1920s	Hoffman makes several summer excursions to Kippewa, Quebec, Canada.
1923	Hoffman sues Salter Path, North Carolina villagers for trespass.
1925	Henry K. Fort sues Salter Path villagers and Alice Hoffman for trespass.

1925	Hoffman sails to China.
1930	Hoffman visits niece Eleanor in Puerto Rico.
1932	Hoffman visits Eleanor in the Philippine Islands.
1933	Hoffman returns to New York City.
1934	Hoffman sails to France.
1938	Hoffman returns to New York City, then moves permanently to Bogue Banks.
1939	Hoffman sues Llewellyn Phillips for fraud. John Marshall Matthias appointed trustee for Hoffman properties.
1940	Hoffman sues Llewellyn Phillips, John Marshall Matthias, the Alden Corporation, and R.N. Lorrimer for fraud.
1942	Hoffman sues Phillips, Matthias, Alden Corp., and Lorrimer again for fraud.
1944	Hoffman sues Llewellyn Phillips for fraud.
1948	Wachovia Bank appointed trustee for Hoffman properties.
1950	Theodore Roosevelt III appointed trustee for Hoffman properties.
1953	Hoffman dies March 15 on Bogue Banks in North Carolina.

APPENDIX C

List of Hoffman's Attorneys

1. John H. Judge, New York City, New York.
2. Herbert L. Satterlee and George F. Canfield, New York City, New York.
3. Arthur H. Haaran, New York City, New York.
4. J.J. Retouret, Paris, France.
5. _______Maugha, Paris, France.
6. Boris Lepkowski, Paris, France.
7. Raymond Harper, New York City, New York.
8. S.S. Szlapka, New York City, New York.
9. Julius F. Duncan, Beaufort, North Carolina.
10. E.H. Gorham, Beaufort, North Carolina.
11. W.C. Gorham, Beaufort, North Carolina.
12. Llewellyn Phillips, Morehead City, North Carolina.
13. John Marshall Matthias, Columbus, Ohio.
14. Frank M. Wooten, Sr., Greenville, North Carolina.
15. Frank M. Wooten, Jr., Greenville, North Carolina.

APPENDIX D

Maps

Railroad Map of North Carolina 1917 Eastern North Carolina

A Portion of Carteret County Second District

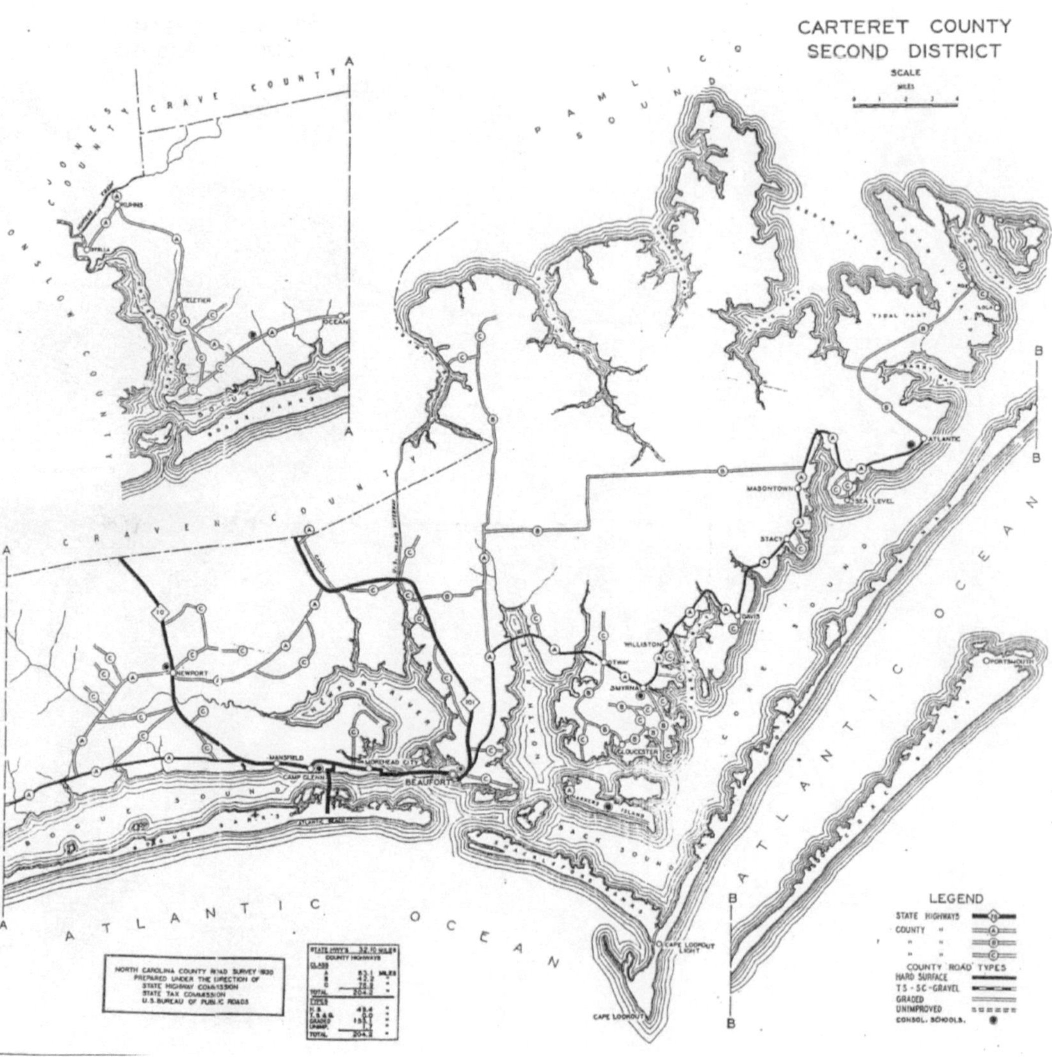

Bogue Banks before the Bridges

BOGUE BANKS BEFORE THE BRIDGES
MAP PREPARED BY JAMES NEWMAN WILLIS III

1923 Judgement Map

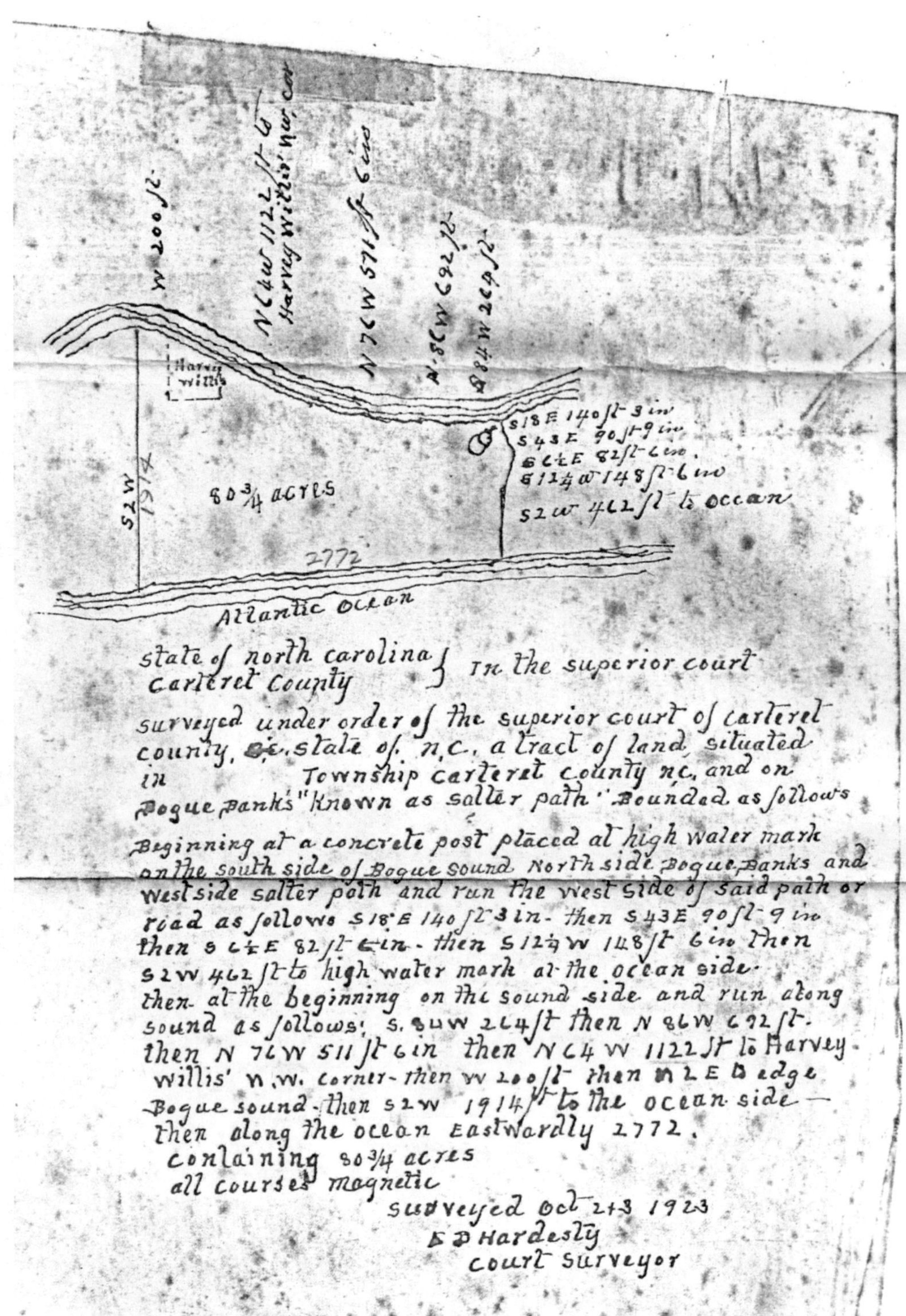

State of North Carolina } In the superior court
Carteret County

Surveyed under order of the superior court of Carteret county, State of N.C., a tract of land situated in Township Carteret County N.C. and on Bogue Banks "known as Salter Path" Bounded as follows

Beginning at a concrete post placed at high water mark on the south side of Bogue Sound North side Bogue Banks and West side Salter Path and run the west side of said path or road as follows S 18° E 140 ft 3 in - then S 43 E 90 ft 9 in then S 6½ E 82 ft 6 in - then S 12¼ W 148 ft 6 in then S 2 W 462 ft to high water mark at the ocean side. Then at the beginning on the sound side and run along sound as follows: S. 84 W 264 ft then N 86 W 692 ft. then N 76 W 511 ft 6 in then N 64 W 1122 ft to Harvey Willis' N.W. corner - then W 200 ft then N 2 E to edge Bogue Sound - then S 2 W 1914 ft to the ocean side — then along the ocean Eastwardly 2772.

Containing 80¾ acres
all courses magnetic

Surveyed Oct 2+3 1923
E D Hardesty
Court Surveyor

APPENDIX E

A Poem in Three Parts,
Part Three

By John E. Matthias

save and except the area described as
follows:

> beginning at the southwest
> corner of the Atlantic Beach
> on the Atlantic Ocean (the
> southeast corner of the
> property known as the Hoffman Property)
> thence running westwardly with
> the Atlantic Ocean waters to
> a point on the ocean two miles
> from the beginning thence northwardly
> and parallel with the west line of
> the Atlantic Beach to the waters
> of Bogue Sound to the
> northwest corner of the Atlantic
> Beach thence with that line which
> is the east line of the Hoffman
> property to the beginning

Save and Except.
Save and Except these lands.
Preserve the Salter Path.
Alice Hoffman not allowed on
the Salter Path. Salter Path
no property of Alice Hoffman.

> Kitty Hawk
> Albemarle Sound
> Manteo
> Roanoke Island

Hatteras
Cape Hatteras
Pamlico Sound
Portsmouth Island
Core Banks
Shackleford Banks
Bogue Banks

approached by sea how
long ago, Davy
John Willis?

Robert Sullivan writes,
circa 1943: "I'd rather go to court than to the
theatre." Thus Mrs. H., circa 1943.

Durham
Raleigh
Goldsboro
New Bern
Morehead City
Beaufort
Bogue Banks

"Beaufort"
"Bowfut"
"Beeoofud"
Bogue Banks

North Carolina for the North Carolinians; Bogue Banks for the Bankers.

(1) *Storm after storm:*
we cannot any longer
hold this course: storm
after storm: Hatteras,
Cope Hatteras, Shackleford
Banks: storm after storm:
food gone: water gone:
men near mutiny:
we cannot any longer
hold this course:
Hatteras, Cape Hatteras,
Shackleford Banks . . .

OUTPOST OF ISOLATION
300 YEARS 300 YEARS
SQUATTERS ON N.CAROLINA
SANDBANK THREATEN VIOLENCE

(2) Through groves of
twisted yaupon trees
to the beach . . . a morning
and an evening haul . . .
barefoot on the sand
and singing, singing . . .
Settlers driven out
of Shackleford by
drifting dunes, out
of Diamond city . . .
Gardens would not grow in the sand,
cattle could not graze, so back (how
many years, John Willis?)
to the sea.

OUTPOST OF ISOLATION
300 YEARS 300 YEARS
SQUATTERS ON N.CAROLINA
SANDBANK THREATEN VIOLENCE

(3) Formal gardens, cultivated
lawns, fountains, arbours,
fancy foreign friends. Once she
brought a harpsichord from
France. Who's the law?
Judge A. Flint. *He* lived a long
time ago. And here we are off
Morehead City Bridge.
Shackleford was sold to the
state, Bogue was sold to
the army. Now we've got
Fort Macon and a missile
base . . .

Did they murder the cooks? Hack
the Butler up? Did they

drink the blood of
the maids?

solid world / measure incomplete

ends and beginnings
cannot be regarded
as fixed

beginning at the southwest
corner of the Atlantic Beach
on the Atlantic Ocean (the
southeast corner of the property
known as the Hoffman Property)
thence running westwardly with
the Atlantic Ocean waters to
a point on the ocean two miles
from the beginning thence northwardly
and parallel with the west line of
the Atlantic Beach to the waters
of Bogue Sound to the
northwest corner of the Atlantic
Beach thence with that line
which is the east line of the
Hoffman Property to the beginning

it is understood and agreed and made a part of this judgement that neither of the parties hereto will interfere in any way with the full exercise of the rights of the other as adjudicated in this instrument and that each of said parties shall be entitled to exercise their rights or privileges as the case may be without interference on the part of the other . . .

Thus the Judge . . .
and under his
breath:
'In the
solid world
measurements
are incomplete.
Time has no
stopping, divisions

have no permanence
and ends and be-
ginnings have no
fixity. The man
of great wisdom
observes both
far and near,
knowing that
measurements are
incomplete. He
is aware of both
fullness and
emptiness so that
he neither rejoices
at life nor thinks
of death as calamity
knowing that ends
and beginnings
cannot be
regarded
as fixed . . .

(save and except the area described
as follows)

beginning at the southwest
corner of the Atlantic Beach
on the Atlantic Ocean (the
southeast corner of the property
known as the Hoffman property) men
with torches knives and other
implements of butchery destruction
desecration did intent on violence
thence run westwardly with Ocean
water to a point on Ocean sands
two miles from beginning and thence
northwardly and parallel with
West Line of Atlantic to the
water of the Bogue and thence
with waters of the Bogue to
northwest corner of Atlantic
Beach and thence along that

line to the beginning and did
terrorize the titled lady
living there (said Mrs. H.) did
rape and ravish slaughter and
profane did catch the chauffeur
cut away his genitals
did murder cooks did hack
the butler up did drink
the blood of pink Parisian maids . . .

BUT

This cause coming on to be heard and being
heard by the court and a jury, the court having
instructed the jury that there was
NO EVIDENCE
NO EVIDENCE

Across Bogue Sound
The Tar-Heels
Saw a Castle
Rise.

Fires there, and each
man with a torch.
Crazy through the
houses
scattered round
the backbone of
the bank. Crazy
up the island nob and down the
Salter Path through
underbrush and
over dunes and
under over-
hanging limbs

Across Bogue Sound
The Tar-Heels
Saw a Jungle
Blaze.

Did they murder the cooks? Hack
the Butler up? Did they
drink the blood of
the maids?

solid world / measure incomplete
ends and beginnings
cannot be regarded
as fixed

. . . whereas there is now pending
in the district court of the United States an
action entitled
United States against 735 acres of land
more or less

Davy John Willis
sits on the beach
and mends nets.

Remembers little.

His ancestors were
pirates.

Mrs. H.
was afraid of him
and of coral snakes . . .

and of the jungle
and of the swamps
and of mosquitoes . . .

(dunes drift, the
sand covers the
crops . . .

And you have been here?
Three Hundred Years.
And your people?
Fish in the sea.

About the Author

Kathleen Guthrie lives in Salter Path, North Carolina, with Douglas, her husband of many years. She has master's degrees in History and English from East Carolina University and even better, three interesting grandchildren, Max, Lucy, and Katy. She thanks God for her life and family. She is an anachronism and a neo-Luddite. She spends her time reading good books, drawing and painting, cleaning, cooking, gardening and doing yardwork, going out in the boat, fishing (with a net), managing a small museum and gallery, and drinking wine with her husband at "winetime" (about 4 p.m.). She urges people to be quiet and to consider the well-being of others around them at all times and places. She asks everyone to regard the importance of the preservation of small villages everywhere in America, so that they will heed where they vacation and commit no nuisance.